# Theological Issues in Christian-Muslim Dialogue

## Edited by Charles Tieszen

☙PICKWICK *Publications* · Eugene, Oregon

THEOLOGICAL ISSUES IN CHRISTIAN-MUSLIM DIALOGUE

Pickwick Publications
An Imprint of Wipf and Stock Publishers
199 W. 8th Ave., Suite 3
Eugene, OR 97401

www.wipfandstock.com

PAPERBACK ISBN: 978-1-5326-1058-5
HARDCOVER ISBN: 978-1-5326-1060-8
EBOOK ISBN: 978-1-5326-1059-2

*Cataloguing-in-Publication data:*

Names: Tieszen, Charles Lowell, 1978–, editor.

Title: Theological issues in Christian-Muslim dialogue / Charles Tieszen.

Description: Eugene, OR : Pickwick Publications, 2018 | Includes bibliographical references.

Identifiers: ISBN 978-1-5326-1058-5 (paperback) | ISBN 978-1-5326-1060-8 (hardcover) | ISBN 978-1-5326-1059-2 (ebook)

Subjects: LCSH: Islam—Relations—Christianity. | Christianity and other religions—Islam.

Classification: BR127 .T5479 2018 (print) | BR127 .T5479 (ebook)

Manufactured in the U.S.A.

*To all those committed to the work of dialogue among Christians and Muslims*

# Contents

# Contributors

**JOHN AZUMAH** is Professor of World Christianity and Islam at Columbia Theological Seminary. His specialties are Islam, Christian-Muslim relations, Christian theology of religions, and missiology and his current research focuses on world Christianity and Islam in the Global South. Professor Azumah is editor or coeditor of several books, including *Christian-Muslim Relations: A Bibliographical History, 1500–1600* (Brill), *The African Christian and Islam* (Langham Monographs), and *Islam and Christianity on the Edge* (Acorn). He is the author of numerous studies in Islam and Christian-Muslim relations including *My Neighbour's Faith* (Hippo) and *The Legacy of Arab-Islam in Africa* (Oneworld).

**MARK BEAUMONT** is Research Associate at London School of Theology. He has published articles on Christian-Muslim relations, especially on theological concerns. He is the author of *Christology in Dialogue with Muslims* (Regnum) and coauthor with Maha El-Kaisy Friemuth of *Al-Radd al-Jamil: A Fitting Refutation of the Divinity of Jesus from the Evidence of the Gospel* (Brill).

**AYŞE İÇÖZ** is Research Assistant at Marmara University in Istanbul. She recently obtained her PhD from the University of Birmingham (England) with a thesis entitled "Christian Morality in the Language of Islam: The Case of al-Masabih Chapter in the Kitab al-Majdal." Currently, she is interested in exploring the development of moral theories in Christian Arabic sources and the ways in which Arabic language was adopted and used by medieval Christian authors as an apologetic tool.

TODD M. JOHNSON is Associate Professor of Global Christianity and Director of the Center for the Study of Global Christianity at Gordon-Conwell Theological Seminary. Dr. Johnson is visiting Research Fellow at Boston University's Institute for Culture, Religion and World Affairs. He is co-editor of the *Atlas of Global Christianity* (Edinburgh University Press) and coauthor of the *World Christian Encyclopedia* (Oxford University Press, 2nd ed.).

SANDRA TOENIES KEATING is Associate Professor of Theology at Providence College, Rhode Island. She specializes in the early centuries of theological exchange between Muslims and Christians and has written numerous articles on this formative period. Currently, she is working on an edition and translation of 'Abd al-Masih al-Kindi's *Apology*. Dr. Keating is a frequent participant in Muslim-Catholic dialogue on a national and international level and has been a Consulter for the Vatican Commission for Religious Relations with Muslims.

LUCINDA ALLEN MOSHER is Faculty Associate in Interfaith Studies at Hartford Seminary, founder-principal of the NeighborFaith Consultancy, and Assistant Academic Director of the Building Bridges Seminar (an international Christian-Muslim dialogue)—for which she coedits its book series. The author of many essays on Islam and Christian-Muslim concerns, she is also coeditor of a special issue of *The Muslim World* on Hindu-Muslim relations.

DOUGLAS PRATT is Professor of Religious Studies at the University of Waikato, New Zealand, and Adjunct Professor in the Faculty of Theology, University of Bern, Switzerland. His research interests include Christian-Muslim relations, interfaith dialogue, and contemporary issues in religion. He has recently published *Religion and Extremism: Rejecting Diversity* (Bloomsbury), *Being Open, Being Faithful: The Journey of Interreligious Dialogue* (World Council Churches), and coedited with Rachel Woodlock *Fear of Muslims? International Perspectives on Islamophobia* (Springer). Professor Pratt's 2005 text, *The Challenge of Islam: Encounters in Interfaith Dialogue*, has been reissued in the Routledge Revival Library.

TARIQ RAMADAN is Professor of Contemporary Islamic Studies at Oxford University, teaching in both the Faculty of Oriental Studies and the Faculty of Theology and Religion. He is also affiliated with the Research Centre of Islamic Legislation and Ethics (CILE) (Doha, Qatar), President of the think-tank European Muslim Network (EMN) in Brussels, and a member of the International Union of Muslim Scholars. Professor Ramadan is author of many works including *Islam: The Essentials* (Pelican Series, Penguin) and *Western Muslims and the Future of Islam* (Oxford University Press). His personal website is www.tariqramadan.com.

Cosmas Ebo Sarbah is Director of Interreligious Dialogue for the Catholic Archdiocese of Cape Coast, founder of the Inter-Faith Youth Core for Muslim and Christian youth in Central Region of Ghana, and, since 2012, a lecturer at both the University of Ghana and St. Peter's Regional Seminary, Pedu. A participant in the annual conferences of the International Conference on Jewish, Christian, and Muslim Relations in Wuppertal, Germany (2007), he also took part in the Study of the U.S. Institute on Religious Pluralism at the University of California, Santa Barbara, in June–July 2016. His articles have appeared in *Studies in Interreligious Dialogue*, *Trinity Journal of Church and Theology*, and the *Journal of Applied Thought*.

Charles Tieszen is SIS Adjunct Professor of Islamic Studies at Fuller Theological Seminary. He is a historian of religious thought with particular interests in the interactions between Muslim and Eastern/Arabized Christian communities. Dr. Tieszen is the author of many works on the history and theology of Christian-Muslim relations including *Cross Veneration in the Medieval Islamic World* (I.B. Tauris), *A Textual History of Christian-Muslim Relations* (Fortress Press), and *Christian Identity amid Islam in Medieval Spain* (Brill). He is also an editor of the forthcoming volumes *Christian-Muslim Relations: A Thematic History* (Brill), part of the series *Christian-Muslim Relations: A Bibliographical History* (Brill).

Pim Valkenberg is Ordinary Professor of Religion and Culture at the School of Theology and Religious Studies, The Catholic University of America in Washington, DC. His main interest is the study of Christian-Muslim relations in the context of Abrahamic partnership. His latest publications include *Renewing Islam by Service: A Christian View of Fethullah Gülen and the Hizmet Movement* (Catholic University of America Press), *Nostra Aetate: Celebrating 50 years of the Catholic Church's Dialogue with Jews and Muslims* (Catholic University of America Press), and *World Religions in Dialogue: A Comparative Theological Perspective* (Anselm Academic).

# Finding Our Way in Christian-Muslim Dialogue

## CHARLES TIESZEN

IT WAS A COOL December morning the first time I drove with my wife and parents to Córdoba, Spain. As we crossed the Guadalquivir River that snakes its way beneath the old city we could see the Mezquita, the former Grand Mosque, in the distance with its Christian cathedral rising from the middle of the complex. Road construction blocked the most direct routes to the Mezquita and the adjacent Hotel Maimonides, our lodging for the night. As a result, we circled the old city several times, searching for an open path amid narrow, winding streets, and making inquiries among Cordobans sipping *café con leche* at street-side cafes. Everyone with whom we spoke was eager to be helpful and each one faithfully provided directions. But these were ultimately of no use; the city was impenetrable to us. My wife and I eventually abandoned the car with my parents remaining inside and proceeded on foot. We returned a bit later with fresh directions to a previously unseen street and an access code to a gate that led us to our final destination. With the car safely parked, we found our way to the Mezquita and explored its many wonders.

It is likely that the Mezquita rests on the site of what was a church dedicated to St. Vincent. In the late eighth century, however, construction began on what would become the Grand Mosque of Córdoba. The church was purchased, destroyed, and subsequent centuries saw multiple expansions to the mosque until it spread out to its current footprint. The interior is a maze of prayer halls and what is ubiquitously—and accurately—described as a "forest" of columns. Much of the Islamic ornamentation and architecture remains to this day, but in 1236 King Ferdinand III of Castile (d. 1252) conquered the city. The mosque was subsequently converted to a Christian church and eventually a Roman Catholic cathedral was built into the middle of the former mosque. Care was taken in many spaces to ensure that structural additions complemented the existing design. So, ecclesiastical architecture often continues the same polychromatic arches and blind arcades of the mosque. In spite of such cases of complementary design, the visual effect leaves one with the sense that the cathedral's architects plunged the structure down onto the mosque in order to dominate it. In fact, one of the church's chapels boasts a statue of *Santiago Matamoros*—St. James the Moor-slayer. In this version, Saint James grasps a sword, not his pilgrim's staff, and raises it above his head. Astride his horse, he tramples over two Muslims.

A great deal of the medieval history of Córdoba can be read in Córdoba's Mezquita. The archeological remnants of the church dedicated to St. Vincent remain on site and many of the mosque's columns are *spolia* of the former church. The mosque's expansions continue to bear witness to the Umayyad caliphate that once grew and flourished. The protruding cathedral reminds onlookers of Christian expansion on the peninsula. Much of the church's architecture, complimentary as it is to the mosque, is testament to the intercommunal harmony between Christian and Muslim (and Jewish) communities. Yet the cathedral's dominance, appearing very nearly as a structural intrusion, suggests to onlookers that, despite intercommunal harmony, one community could be made in various ways to feel subservient to another.

As with the Mezquita, so might it also be said of the intricacies of Christian-Muslim encounter. History is replete with examples of cooperation and cross-fertilization, of examples where adherents of one community received care, inspiration, or companionship from adherents of the other. Even so, examples of antagonism, dominance, and even violence between the two communities abound as well. Navigating one's way through the ambiguities of this history, much like Córdoba's city streets, can be daunting. At times, inroads seem out of reach and the prospect of productive dialogue elusive.

Beyond the Mezquita, the city of Córdoba continues to evoke the challenges and opportunities present in Christian-Muslim encounter. In March 1977, representatives from both religious communities gathered in the city for the Second International Muslim-Christian Congress. During one session, Gregorio Ruiz attempted to answer the question, "In what sense can

Muhammad be considered a prophet by Christians?"[1] For Ruiz, the term "prophet" had a very broad meaning. It could even take on a sociological sense in which "one revolts against his environment and despite its hostility is able to influence it."[2] In this way, according to Ruiz, one could consider Karl Marx (1818–1883) a prophet and Ruiz had little problem affirming this sociological aspect of Muhammad's prophethood.[3] According to conference reports, these comments were "listened to in complete silence, as if heralding a storm. The reactions from the Muslim side came quickly."[4] In the end, Ruiz clarified his remarks and attendees agreed to "look for a solution in harmony with [the] spirit of the congress."[5] Similarly, like the Mezquita whose architecture evokes at once both communal harmony and discord, Christian-Muslim dialogue risks confusion. At times, it can seem impenetrable and one's best path toward clarity can often only be found after consulting the proper guides who can offer the best guidance.

This book offers guidance to readers who are scholars, practitioners, or those simply interested in Christian-Muslim dialogue. The focus of authors who contributed essays is primarily theological; the chapters comprise the most common, and most important, theological topics that emerge when Christians and Muslims encounter one another in religious discussion. Similarly, these topics are also the most enduring since one can find Christians and Muslims discussing them in nearly every century since the inception of Islam. Christians and Muslims continue, for example, to discuss the nature of God as strictly one or as Trinity-in-Unity, the nature of prophethood and revelation, the nature of humanity, and the formation and enrichment of community. Theological reflection, therefore, must continue to be brought to bear on these topics in light of their history and in view of their continual applicability in contexts of interreligious engagement.

While this book can stand on its own in this effort, it also has a complementary function. It exists as a companion to a collection of primary sources I compiled in *A Textual History of Christian-Muslim Relations* (Minneapolis: Fortress, 2015). In that book, readers are introduced

---

1. See a report of the congress by Galindo Aguilar, "The Second International Muslim-Christian Congress of Cordoba," 161–83.

2. Ibid., 168.

3. Troll, "Muhammad—Prophet auch für Christen?" 294. See also, Troll, *Dialogue and Difference*, 119–20.

4. Galindo Aguilar, 168.

5. Ibid., 169.

to many of the most important primary sources written by Christians and Muslims about one another's religion. The theological topics that emerge in these texts are brought into focus in the present volume, placed into contemporary contexts of Christian-Muslim dialogue in which they continue to be discussed, and given rigorous theological analysis. I hope the result, both in this book and along with its companion volume, is a substantial sourcebook for readers learning about Christian-Muslim relations and practitioners engaged in Christian-Muslim dialogue.

One of the most enduring topics in the history of Christian-Muslim dialogue was the nature of God, and of particular concern was the question of whether God should be described as Trinity-in-Unity—and what exactly such a formula meant—or strictly one. This debate continues in the present day, but a new and related question emerged at the very beginning of the twenty-first century that does not have significant historical precedent: do Christians and Muslims worship the same God? This is not a question that most Muslims ask, for Islam is built upon the idea that the Qur'an was revealed to correct and revive monotheistic worship of the one God, the God of Abraham, Isaac, Jacob, and Jesus.

The matter could be quite different for Christians. That this question does not appear in their historical texts is likely the result of a certain set of assumptions. A writer might assume, for example, that Muslims were idolaters and there are texts, particularly from the medieval Latin West, in which Muslims are accused of worshiping various gods or even of worshiping Muhammad.[6] But such accusations or assessments are usually based upon an inadequate understanding of Islam. Many other texts, especially those from Eastern Christians, include theological discussions that assume the Allah of Islam was the God of Christianity. Arabic-speaking Christians, after all, said and wrote "Allah" when they spoke of the Triune God, just as they do today. Even those writing in Syriac could write that Muslims knew the one true God, even if they thought Muslims did so imperfectly.[7] There are a few examples to the contrary and one thinks of an anonymous author writing in Arabic in the ninth century, answering a question about whether or not Muslims and Christians might together affirm the first clause of the Islamic creed (shahada)—"I witness that there is no God but the God" (ashadu an

---

6. For some analysis of this kind of charge of idolatry, see Kinoshita and Calkin, "Saracens as Idolaters in European Vernacular Literatures."

7. See, for example, an anonymous author's account of a disputation between an East-Syrian Christian monk and a Muslim, the text and translation of which appears in Taylor, "The Disputation between a Muslim and a monk of Bet Hale."

*la ilaha illa Allah*). The author's answer comes in a sharp condemnation and his conclusion is that "by 'there is no god but God' [Muslims] mean a god other than the Father, the Son, and the Holy Spirit."[8] This kind of statement, however, is rare in Arabophone texts written by Christians. When it does appear, it often seems the case, as with this ninth-century author, that there is a concern for identity politics—an effort to delineate members of one religious community over and against members of another one—not necessarily a careful theological articulation of the nature of God in Islam and Christianity.[9]

Identity politics, rather than theology, strictly speaking, may in fact be the primary motivator behind the modern question about whether or not Muslims and Christians worship the same God. Pim Valkenberg begins our theological reflection in chapter 1 by applying both historical and theological analysis to the question in order to argue that the ways in which this question are posed are not all helpful. He offers a different framework for considering what Muslims and Christians know, or do not know, about the One God.

In chapter 2, Sandra Toenies Keating takes up the topic of the Holy Spirit, in particular the identity of the Paraclete and the Muslim argument that this figure indicated the Prophet Muhammad. This was a very common discussion in medieval disputational and apologetic literature and it continues to appear in contemporary contexts, even taking on, as Keating addresses, new forms of justification. Keating's discussion of the Paraclete in the context of Christian-Muslim relations also leads her to address the Islamic doctrine of *tahrif*, the idea that somehow Jewish and Christian Scriptures became or were deliberately corrupted. Keating situates the development of this doctrine in the contexts of debates over the identity of the Paraclete and offers a way forward in the midst of what might otherwise seems to be an intractable dispute.

Keating's chapter also raises the question of how Christians ought to view the prophethood of Muhammad. Was he someone other prophets, including Jesus, foretold? Historically, Christians debated how they ought to assess Muhammad and the Muslim claims about his prophethood. Some dismissed him outright while others suggested he served some kind of

8. Quoted in Hoyland, "St. Andrews Ms. 14 and the Earliest Arabic *Summa Theologiae*," 166. See also, Griffith, *The Church in the Shadow of the Mosque*, 58.

9. See Tieszen, *Cross Veneration in the Medieval Islamic World*, 105–12. For ways in which religious identity can incorporate theological, sociological, and political concerns, see Tieszen, *Christian Identity amid Islam in Medieval Spain*.

prophetic function for Arabs, pointing them towards monotheism. Neither of these conclusions, of course, is satisfactory for Muslims who see Muhammad as God's final messenger sent with a universal message. With this in mind, Mark Beaumont analyzes in chapter 3 many of the theories put forth by scholars and considers how Christians might view the prophethood of Muhammad by placing the complex matter in the context of how Christians understand prophecy.

One of the things that becomes clear in Beaumont's chapter is that an understanding of prophecy is critical to how Christians can understand Muhammad and, in turn, how Muslims view Jesus. In chapter 4, Tariq Ramadan makes even more explicit the importance of how prophecy is understood in the Muslim and Christian traditions. His discussion reveals that the Islamic view of Jesus is not simply a denial of Christian dogmatic claims, but a corrective that makes a view of Jesus consistent with the Islamic view of messengers and prophets. This distinction helps to guide the ways Muslims and Christians might disagree over the functions of Jesus and Muhammad, but Ramadan also helps to point out the way an Islamic understanding of prophecy, and Jesus' role in that, can draw Muslims and Christians together.

If the nature of prophecy is a concept in which Muslims and Christians might disagree, then the concept of revelation is also an area where the two religions depart. On the one hand, both Islam and Christianity agree that God revealed something to humanity. For Muslims, on the one hand, God revealed his will in the Qur'an, a book sent down in pure Arabic. As a result of this kind of verbal revelation, the Qur'an loses its essence when it is translated out of Arabic. Versions of the Qur'an in other languages are not translations, strictly speaking, but interpretations. For Christians, on the other hand, God revealed himself in the person of Jesus Christ. In the Christian view, it is the person of Christ, not a divine book, which is the apex of divine revelation. In this light, appreciating the distinctions in revelation is paramount in Christian-Muslim dialogue.

Not everyone engaged in Christian-Muslim dialogue, however, has always appreciated these nuances, as Ayşe İçöz shows in chapter 5 on how the Qur'an was understood to function in the context of Christian-Muslim encounters. As İçöz points out, there were times when Christian authors were aware of the impact the Qur'an had on Muslims. Some, for example, were well aware of the internal Muslim debates about the createdness of the Qur'an. Various authors used this knowledge to their advantage in apologetics. Others, either unaware of the intricacies of how Muslims view the Qur'an and revelation or simply willing to ignore them, favor their own interpretations of the Qur'an that support apologetic or missiological purposes.

John Azumah follows in chapter 6 with a Christian understanding of revelation, the role Jesus plays as God's revelation in particular. He makes clear that some of the central differences between Islam and Christianity on this topic center on the nature and function of revelation. But in the depths of these differences can be found some important and unique common ground. And, as Azumah makes clear, the differences between Muslims and Christians on the matter of revelation can be fodder for our most productive dialogue.

Chapter 7 marks a shift in focus away from divinity, revelation, and text toward humanity. Cosmas Ebo Sarbah considers in this chapter the human condition and how Christians and Muslims conceive of the notion of sin and, in turn, redemption. The subtle nuances present in this concept were particularly cumbersome in the history of Christian-Muslim dialogue. Many Christians, especially those affirming the notion of original sin, were keen to view humanity as inherently sinful and in need of a savior. Muslims, however, do not view human nature in the same way and the need for a savior, at least in the way Christians view Christ and the cross, is superfluous, not to mention inappropriately scandalous in view of their understanding of prophethood. Much theology, then, can diverge from this point of difference between Christianity and Islam. But as Sarbah shows, our views on the human condition and the need to somehow redemptively address this condition can draw Christians and Muslims together as well.

Chapter 8 continues a focus on humanity where Lucinda Allen Mosher considers how Christians and Muslims view the formation and maintenance of religious communities. Historically, many Muslims were quick to exploit the apparent disunity evident in various Christian traditions, often times based on differing theologies. Christian authors did likewise when it came to apparent Islamic disunity. Mosher's contribution examines the realities of this disunity as well as the ways in which Christians and Muslims conceive of the ideals of unity in their traditions. Significantly, Mosher draws our attention back to the fundamental distinctions found within Islamic and Christian conceptions of revelation and how these shape views of community.

In chapter 9, Douglas Pratt brings us beyond topics that are rooted in historic discussions. Religious pluralism and dialogue, the focus of his chapter, are not viewed in the same manner in contemporary contexts as they were in the medieval period. In this light, Pratt helps us consider the implications that the realties of religious pluralism, both globally and locally, have upon efforts in Christian-Muslim dialogue. Most significantly, he helps us see the importance of dialogue. Even though many of the theological topics discussed in this book have persisted for well over a millennium, the work of dialogue, and theological dialogue in particular, remains necessary.

Finally, Todd Johnson concludes our theological reflection by looking ahead and marking out some trends in religious demography that help us speculate on the future of Christian-Muslim relations. For centuries, Christianity was almost inextricably linked with the West. Similarly, "Islam" is often reduced to a category and made to cover its own set of assumed geography. In fact, adherents of Christian populations are growing largely outside of the western and northern hemispheres, outside of traditionally "Christian" areas. Statistically speaking, the "center" of Christianity actually lies in the Global South. Muslims, most of whom are not Arabic speakers, are also seeing growth in their religious communities outside of traditionally Islamic areas like the Middle East.[10] For these reasons alone, the notion of "Islam and the West" is deeply problematic and an insufficient construct in which to frame Christian-Muslim relations. Productive dialogue demands that we do better and be more precise. Johnson's closing essay helps us understand what may be at stake demographically and suggests a few guideposts for the way ahead that will help to shape theological reflection and dialogue.

A few technical notes on language and chronology are worth sharing here. In many works devoted to Islamic studies that are written in English, a system of transliteration using Latin characters represents Arabic letters and vowel markings. In this book, a very simplified system of transliteration is used whereby Arabic words (and, indeed, words in Greek, Hebrew, and other languages) are simply italicized and rendered into English without diacritical marks. The Arabic letter *ayn* is represented with a ' and the *hamza* is represented with a '. Common Arabic words like "Muhammad" or "Qur'an" are transliterated according to this simple style, but they are left unitalicized.

---

10. Johnson and Ross, eds., *Atlas of Global Christianity*, 8–9, 10–11.

Books that deal in various ways with Islam also frequently refer to the Islamic Hijri calendar. In order to ease the reader's work in reading this book, I have also simplified dates so that they all reflect the Common Era. If a date precedes the Common Era, then it is followed by "BCE."

Finally, I have not included the Arabic titles of chapters in the Qur'an, instead choosing to use a simple number-and-verse reference style preceded by a "Q" (for Qur'an, in order to distinguish between biblical references). For example, a reference to the first verse (*aya*) of the first chapter (*sura*) of the Qur'an, *al-Fatiha*, would appear as "Q 1:1."

# God in Muslim and Christian Thought

## PIM VALKENBERG

IN A BOOK THAT gives an overview of theological issues in Christian-Muslim dialogue, it seems quite natural to start with God. After all, both Christians and Muslims start their attestations of faith by declaring that they believe in one God. "We believe in one God" (*pisteuomen eis hena theon*) are the first words of the Creed accepted by the councils of Nicaea (325) and Constantinople (381). Similarly, the Muslim proclamation of faith begins with the words "I witness that there is no deity except (the one who is) God" (*ashadu an la ilaha illa Allah*). Yet at the same time it is evident that Christians and Muslims approach their God in deeply different ways, summarized as *tawhid* (saying that God is One) for Muslims, and Trinity (saying that God is Triune) for Christians. So how do the oneness of God and the different approaches to God in the two religions go together? Do we together worship the one true God or not?

In this chapter I will try to elaborate on these questions from a historical and systematic point of view. I will begin by discussing a few central verses in the Qur'an because this is where the dialogue between Christians and Muslims takes its point of departure. I will continue by discussing the largely apologetic and antagonistic contributions by Christian and Muslim theologians. Finally, I want to highlight some of the contemporary dialogues between Christians and Muslims about the question as to whether we worship the same God. I hope to show that there are different ways to phrase this question and that not all of these are equally helpful.

## The Qur'an: Your God and Our God Is One

Among the texts in the Qur'an that form the basis for much later dialogue between Muslims and Christians, two texts have a special importance because they contain instructions both on the form of this dialogue and on its contents. Moreover, modern Muslim scholars consider these two texts as the most important foundations for dialogue among the Abrahamic religions.[1]

The first text admonishes the Prophet Muhammad (c. 570–632) and his followers in an early stage of the development of their community to discuss matters of faith with Jews and Christians as "People of Scripture" (*Ahl al-Kitab*), recognizing their status as religions based on a Scripture sent down by God to specific messengers.[2] Even though the verb "argue" (*jadala*) used in the text foreshadows debate as one of the primary methods of communication between Muslims and Christians, the text adds that this debate needs to be done in the best possible way, provided that the partners are sincere in faith and ethics. The text says the following: "And do not argue with the People of the Scripture unless it be in (a way) that is better, except with such of them as do wrong; and say: 'We believe in that which has been revealed to us and revealed to you; our God and your God is One, and to Him we surrender'" (Q 29:46).[3] This text shows two areas in which fruitful communication between the believers and the People of Scripture is possible. First of all, there is considerable commonality between the revelations to Jews and Christians and the revelation to Muhammad and his companions. Therefore, mutual consultation concerning the scriptures that are the audible and visible result of these revelations is not only possible but also maybe even required for a better understanding of them. Second, there is not only commonality but also identification in the source of these revelations: our God and your God is one. This is not only a mathematical equation (there is only one God) but it leads to identical behavior: we align ourselves to God. The last word of the quotation, *muslimun*, is usually translated as "we submit [to God]" and it has almost everywhere in the

---

1. See Kurucan and Erol, *Dialogue in Islam*, 34–35.

2. On the early believers' movement, their basic beliefs, and their relation to the People of Scripture, see Donner, *Muhammad and the Believers*, 56–74.

3. Translation based on Muhammad Marmaduke Pickthall's translation in "Meaning of the Glorious Qur'an," 212. Angelika Neuwirth states that this text is chronologically the first text to mention the People of Scripture. See Neuwirth, *Koran als Text der Spätantike*, 144.

Qur'an an inclusive meaning: it does not only include Muslims, but others who focus their lives on God and conduct themselves accordingly.[4]

The second text that is important in this context is the famous "common word" verse that addresses the People of Scripture as follows: "Say: 'O People of the Book! Come to an agreement between us and you: that we shall worship none but God, and that we shall ascribe no partner to Him, and that none of us shall take others for lords beside God.' And if they turn away, then say: 'Bear witness that we are they who have surrendered (to Him)'" (Q 3:64).[5] This text, believed to be revealed in Medina on the occasion of a visit by a delegation of Christians from Najran near the Yemen, proposes the same basic statement as an agreement (or "common word") to these Christians: that we worship none but God, and ascribe no partner to Him. It is possible to read this as a statement that both Muslims and Christians could endorse, and it is this reading that has been promoted by the Muslim scholars and religious leaders who signed the "A Common Word" document in 2007.[6] Yet, at the same time the text has polemical connotations as well, since it contains two further conditions explaining what it means to worship none but God: not sharing (*sharaka*) God's divinity with anything, and not taking one another as lords (*arbab*) beside God. It is very well possible to give an interpretation of these conditions that shows how the Christian Trinitarian faith is not affected by them; first, by pointing out that faith in the Triune God does indeed not imply sharing God's divinity with anything else, and second by pointing out that it does not lead to accepting human beings as lords. This is the interpretation that the signatories of "A Common Word" give, supported by the famous qur'anic exegete Abu Ja'far Muhammad ibn Jarir al-Tabari (d. 923).[7]

However, if one reads this verse in its entirety, it seems that its latter part indicates disagreement rather than agreement: "if they turn away, say 'Bear witness that we are *muslimun*.'" Such an "agreement to disagree" would fit very well with the historical context for this verse according to the Islamic tradition of "occasions of the revelations" that tries to connect certain verses in the Qur'an with certain events in the life of the Prophet

4. See Donner, *Muhammad and the Believers*, 71.

5. Translated in Pickthall, "Meaning of the Glorious Qur'an," 33.

6. A wealth of information is represented on the website devoted to the "A Common Word" document, hosted by the Royal *Aal al-Bayt* Institute for Islamic Thought at www. acommonword.com. For a printed version, see Volf et al., eds., *Common Word*, 28–50.

7. See ibid., 47.

Muhammad and his companions. 'Ali ibn Ahmad Al-Wahidi (d. 1075), the most famous representative of this "occasions of the revelations" genre connects the first part of the third sura with a visit of a delegation of Christians from Najran—an area in the south of the Arabian Peninsula, close to present-day Yemen—to the Prophet Muhammad and his community in Medina. While the Prophet offered them hospitality and allowed them to pray in his mosque, the Christians remained convinced that they were the true *muslimun* because they had accepted faith in the true God. Muhammad, however, claimed that being truly devoted to God excludes giving companions to God, and therefore Jesus cannot be the Son of God. He proposed to invoke God's rejection on those who did not speak the truth—the *mubahala*, or ordeal associated with Q 3:61—but the Christians decided not to risk their lives and went back to Najran.[8]

If we accept this story as historical background of the "common word" verse, it expresses disagreement rather than commonality, both as to the identity of true believers and as to the way in which God should be approached. In fact, later exegetes such as the influential politician Sayyid Abul A'la Mawdudi (d. 1979) characterize the "common word" verse as "an invitation . . . for the two parties to agree on something believed in by one of them, the Muslims, and the soundness of which could hardly be denied by the other party, the Christians."[9] Such an interpretation matches with a situation in which Christians recognize the political superiority of an Islamic government by paying the *jizya* tax (a tax sometimes levied against non-Muslim subjects in many medieval and late-modern Muslim societies), as the likely outcome of the "common word" debate according to al-Wahidi. Yet it is possible to interpret the "common word" verse in a way that leaves space for two faith communities to each develop their own "word of justice" or "equitable word."[10]

On the basis of these two texts it can be said that the Qur'an asserts that Christians and Muslims worship one God, yet the right worship of God would be incomplete without acceptance of the revelations that God has bestowed on humankind, and promotion of justice in human relationships. This threefold theological claim is addressed specifically at the People of Scripture in places such as Q 42:15. Faith in the one God will also guarantee

---

8. Guezzou, *Al-Wahidi's Asbab al-Nuzul*, 44–49.

9. Mawdudi, *Towards Understanding the Qur'an*, 262n57.

10. I have developed this further in "Common Word or a Word of Justice?" (forthcoming).

reward with God for Christians, Jews, and some others if it goes together with faith in the Last Day and acting righteously.[11]

Yet, at the same time the Qur'an points out very clearly that Christians go wrong when they say "three" (Q 4:171) or when they say that "Christ is the Son of God" (Q 9:30). The most incisive critique of what it brandishes as Christian waywardness comes at the end of the fifth sura when God engages in an imaginary dialogue with Christ and asks him if he did indeed say "take me and my mother as two gods alongside God" (Q 5:116). Jesus denies ever having said such a thing and assures that he is faithful to what God has commanded him to say: "Worship God, my Lord and your Lord" (Q 5:117). So it is clear that the Qur'an asserts that there are severe problems with the way in which Christians worship the one God, and yet these problems arise on the basis of a common acknowledgement that there is but one God.[12]

## Historical Encounters: No Polemics without Commonalities

The first impression that one gets when leafing through some recent anthologies of Christian–Muslim historical encounters is that even at an early stage representatives of both religious traditions were able to communicate their theological points of view quite effectively.[13] Specifically in works of early *kalam* ("apologetic" or "speculative theology") literature, there is a deep mutual understanding between Christian scholars and Muslim scholars about the nature of theology as God-talk. They speak at length about God's nature and God's names, God's actions and God's attributes in ways that clearly presuppose mutual understanding of what they say, even if they ultimately do not agree.[14] Of course the general tendency of these texts was

11. See Q 2:62 and, almost identical, Q 5:69.

12. The problems of the Qur'an with Christian approaches to the one God are related to both the incarnation and Trinitarian theology. Since the role of Jesus will be discussed in later chapters, I concentrate on the Trinitarian aspects in this chapter.

13. See the texts in Siddiqui, ed., *Routledge Reader*; Tieszen, *A Textual History of Christian-Muslim Relations*; and a broader array of texts, but from a more specific tradition in Penn, *When Christians First Met Muslims*.

14. It is no coincidence that many early apologetic and polemical texts discuss *tawhid* and Trinity. See the texts by Theodore Abu Qurrah (in Tieszen, *Textual History*, 35–45), Abu Ra'itah (ibid., 60–70), 'Abd al-Masih al-Kindi (ibid., 78–84), Abu 'Isa al-Warraq (ibid., 86–97), al-Jubba'i (ibid., 116–20), al-Maturidi (ibid., 121–26), and al-Baqillani (ibid., 127–34).

polemical, but a polemical text can only be effective if it is based on a sufficient understanding of the point of view of the adversary addressed.[15] In this respect, the reference to the One God functions as a framework within which mutual critique is formulated.

In his "Heresy of the Ishmaelites," John of Damascus (d. 749) uses quite strong words to express his disdain for Muhammad: he is a false prophet who devised his own heresy and wrote ridiculous things in a book that he composed while claiming that it came from God. Yet at the same time John acknowledges that Muhammad brought the Arabs from idolatry to monotheism.[16] In a similar way, the Muslim theologian 'Abd al-Jabbar (d. 1025) strikes a very polemical tone in his "Critique of Christian Origins," but his criticism is based on an extensive knowledge of Christian doctrines and sects.[17] The problem, however, with polemical texts such as these is that the tendency to enlarge the differences between the two traditions makes it rather difficult to notice that both traditions have one ultimately reality in view.[18] I therefore propose to start outside the polemical engagement in order to get a better point of departure.[19]

## Thomas Aquinas and God's Simpleness

When we compare Thomas Aquinas (d. 1274) to John of Damascus or 'Abd al-Jabbar, it becomes immediately clear that this Dominican friar from the thirteenth century knows almost nothing about Islam as a religion. Reading his discussion of Muhammad in the sixth chapter of the first book of the *Summa contra Gentiles* is almost an embarrassing experience, and even though his discussion of a handful of Muslim objections against the Christian faith in *De rationibus fidei* is somewhat more theological in nature, it

15. See Hettema and van der Kooij, eds., *Religious Polemics in Context*. With reference to the Qur'an, see Sirry, *Scriptural Polemics*; and Azaiez, *Le contre-discours coranique*.

16. John of Damascus and his "Heresy of the Ishmaelites" are discussed in Davids and Valkenberg, "John of Damascus," 18–32 and in Tieszen, *Textual History*, 15–19.

17. Text and translation in 'Abd al-Jabbar, *Critique of Christian Origins*; partial translation in Tieszen, *Textual History*, 135–41.

18. In his *Understanding Christian-Muslim Relations*, Bennett makes a distinction between conciliatory and confrontational approaches. Even though there have been notable exceptions, it is fair to say that the history of Christian-Muslim relations has been dominated by confrontational approaches.

19. This proposal is somewhat similar to the intriguing proposal by Cutsinger in his chapter "Disagreeing to Agree."

remains true that Aquinas is not prepared to engage with Islam theologically.[20] Yet in his systematic writings he reflects on the language that we use when talking about God, which might be one way to look differently at the usual opposition between monotheistic and Trinitarian faith.[21] This opposition seems to be alluded at when the Qur'an summons Christians "not to exceed in their religion" and "not to say 'three'" (Q 4:171). This seems to suggest that Christians use "three" (*thalatha*) as a slogan, over against Muslims who use "one" as a slogan, and thus make *tawhid* ("to say 'one'") their distinctive point of view.

Aquinas, however, makes clear that our language about God is not about numbers but about expressing the fundamental distinction between God and everything else that exists.[22] The word that best expresses how God is different is not oneness but simpleness.[23] If we want to know how God is, we first need to discern how God is not by removing from God whatever is fundamental for everything else, i.e., compositeness. Therefore, Aquinas discusses this simpleness as a first and fundamental indication for how God is different from everything else. This "negative approach" is necessary since we cannot know how God is, but rather we know how God is not.[24] So, the consideration of the lack of any compositeness in God serves a purpose similar to the Islamic profession that there is no deity except God. From this point of departure Aquinas concludes that God cannot enter into any form of composition with anything, thus excluding any form of *shirk* (sharing divinity).[25] Even more importantly, God cannot belong to a genus, so there is no general category of "deity" of which the God confessed by Christians would be a specific instantiation.[26] This yields a rule of speaking that is to my mind of utmost importance in Christian-Muslim relationships: *Deus non est in aliquo genere;* "God does not belong to a genus." This does not only imply that it makes no sense to speak about "the Muslim God" or "the Christian God," but also that it makes no sense

---

20. I have discussed this in Valkenberg, "Can We Talk Theologically?"

21. See Burrell, *Aquinas.*

22. On this fundamental distinction, see Sokolowski, *God of Faith and Reason.*

23. Aquinas, *Summa theologiae* I q.3.

24. Aquinas, prologue to *Summa theologiae,* I q.3: *quia de Deo scire non possumus quid sit sed quid non sit, non possumus considerare de Deo quomodo sit sed potius quomodo non sit.*

25. Aquinas, *Summa theologiae,* I q.3 a.8.

26. Ibid., I q.3 a.5.

to ask whether Muslims and Christians worship "the same God," since the category of sameness implies a genus that does not exist.

The fact that many of the insights derived from Aquinas seem to be relevant for both Christians and Muslims in their reflections on God is no coincidence. Historically speaking, Aquinas derived much of his analysis of human God-talk and of the infinite distance between the Creator and all creatures from Islamic and Jewish sources.[27] It is indeed the insight into the decisive distinction between Creator and creatures that forms the common background of this universal form of monotheism: there can be only one Creator of heaven and earth, and this Creator is the only One who exists of necessity, while everything else is dependent for its existence on this Creator.

There is, however, a shadow side to this form of monotheism as well. If Christians think that there is only one God, and if they think that Muslims do not sincerely worship that one God, they must come to the conclusion that they worship a perversion or denial of the one true God. The usual way in which Christians have expressed this was to say that Muslims worship the devil, or that Islam was an instrument of the Antichrist. Another way was to say that Muhammad received his inspiration not from God but from heretics, because he did not tell the truth but invented lies about God.[28] Even though it is easy to see how such expressions could lead to demonizing Islam and its prophet, they start from the basic presupposition that Christianity and Islam relate to the One God albeit differently as day and night.

## Trinitarian Theology and the Politics of Identity

It seems that the form of monotheism that Aquinas has sketched in the first part of his *Summa theologiae* is quite abstract and far removed from a specifically Christian approach that takes into account that God, according to the large majority of Christians, is not only simple but also Trinitarian. Indeed, there seems to be a chasm between the discussion of God as One in *Summa theologiae*, I 1–26 and his discussion of God as Triune in *Summa*

27. For more details, see Burrell, *Knowing the Unknowable God*; and Arnaldez, *A la croisée des trois monothéismes*.

28. Both arguments can be found in John of Damascus' text about the "Heresy of the Ishmaelites" (see translations in Davids and Valkenberg, 19–21 and Tieszen, *Textual History*, 16–19).

*theologiae*, I 27–43. And yet, Aquinas would insist that the one God is the Triune and vice versa; the difference is in our way of approaching God.[29]

It is also true that the rather philosophical approach that I have described is not the only possible approach for a Christian or a Muslim. It is not difficult to find language about God, for example in the book that Christians call the Old Testament, in which God seems to be specifically related to a special group, for instance "the God of Israel" or "the God of Abraham, Isaac, and Jacob." Sometimes, this leads to language in which "our God" is contrasted with "your God" or "their God." Nowadays, such language is often used in situations in which believers or scholars are fearful that the differences between religions are overlooked in expressions such as "Abrahamic religions" or "monotheistic religions" or "religions of the book."[30] In order to preserve the specific identity of one religion, they tend to speak about "the Christian God" over against "the Muslim God," or "*Allah*" over against "God."[31] Even though I share the desire of these authors to safeguard the specific identity of Christianity and Islam, I fear that their proposals lead to a form of theology that is contaminated by identity politics. The most evident contemporary example of such an identity politics is the verdict of a Malaysian court in 2013 that Christians cannot use the word *Allah* to refer to God in their religion. Even though quite a few Christians would agree that the "God of the Bible" cannot be the same as "*Allah*," there are some good theological arguments against such an opposition.[32] Another way to discover the identity politics behind the choice of words is to compare different translations of the meanings of the Qur'an in English: authors who tend to stress the differences between Islam and other religions tend to leave the Arabic word *Allah* untranslated, while those who stress the common points between Islam and other religions tend to translate this word as "God."[33]

In the context of dialogue between Christians and Muslims, it is very important to reflect on the nature of our language concerning God. My own experience in the Netherlands in the 1990s was that it was precisely in dialogue with Muslims that it became clear to me that I should focus more

29. See Long, *Perfectly Simple Triune God.*

30. See Brague, "Concept of the Abrahamic Religions."

31. Some examples (from very different perspectives): Brague, *Du Dieu des chrétiens*; Hughes, *Abrahamic Religions*; Ireland, *Inviting Muslims to Christ.*

32. See McAnnally-Linz and Volf, "God and Allah"; Volf, *Allah.*

33. See Lawrence, *Who Is Allah?*, 16–17.

and more on what it means for Christians to worship a Triune God, and to talk about this God in Trinitarian language. Together with excellent theologians such as Karl Rahner and Jacques Dupuis, I also think that Trinitarian theology may give Christians the best frame of reference to talk about their relations with other religions, specifically Islam.[34] And yet, I am also aware that Trinitarian theology has often been used by Christians as a way to highlight their differences with others, specifically Jews and Muslims. If this is done in order to honestly explain the provenance of Christian language of faith, it is necessary and indispensable in any theological dialogue. Yet if Trinitarian language is used in order to avoid a theological exchange by proclaiming that no common ground is possible because no god is like the Trinitarian God, I argue that this is not a proper theological use but a form of identity politics.[35] Again, a short reference to an analogical situation might help here: in the discussions about the spiritual foundations of the European civilization after September 11, 2001, quite a few right-wing politicians (among them Dutch politicians Pim Fortuyn, Frits Bolkestein and Ayaan Hirsi Ali) appealed to Jewish-Christian values in order to exclude Islam from this European heritage.[36] Such a hyphenation of two religions is suspect if it is meant to exclude a third religion and its claim to be part of the same Abrahamic heritage.

## Lessons from the Dialogue with Jews

The inclusion of Judaism as a third partner in the dialogue between Christians and Muslims may serve to make clear that Christians tend to relate differently to these two partners. Some authors explain this difference by appealing to anthropological and sociological laws according to which the older religion defends its claims against the newer religion, while the newer religion can only establish itself by critiquing the older religion in a form of supersessionism.[37] Since Christianity is in the middle position

34. See Rahner, "Einzigkeit und Dreifaltigkeit Gottes"; Dupuis, *Toward a Christian Theology*; and Valkenberg, "Christian Identity."

35. Volf is to be commended for his careful analysis of such misuse of Trinitarian language to avoid true dialogue with Muslims. See his *Allah*.

36. See Prins, *Voorbij de onschuld*. A similar analysis is in Nussbaum, *New Religious Intolerance*.

37. See Lambert, *Le Dieu distribué*; and Reuven Firestone, *Who Are the Real Chosen People?*

of the three genealogically related "Abrahamic" faiths, it can acknowledge the older tradition of Judaism as part of its own history—even though it confirms this faith precisely as older and thus superseded—but it does not acknowledge the claim of the newer tradition of Islam. The decision to keep the Hebrew Bible as part of the biblical canon, together with the growing awareness that Jesus and his disciples were Jews, means that Christianity needs Judaism in order to understand its own origins. Yet it needed the atrocity of the *Shoah* to engage in a meaningful dialogue with living Jews.

Conversely, until very recently the Qur'an has never been acknowledged as a source of revelation for Christians, nor was Muhammad ever widely recognized as a prophet from God. Muslims usually see this as a lack of insight or fairness since they claim to honor Jesus as a prophet, and in principle they validate the Torah and the Gospel as revelations from God—although in practice the doctrine of *tahrif*, or corruption, prevents them from consulting these revelations in the form in which Jews and Christians have preserved them.[38] This means that most Christians think—for some good theological reasons—that they have much more in common with Jews than with Muslims. For that reason, they usually do not feel the need to insist on Trinitarian language because they accept that Christians and Jews worship one God, even though Jews do not accept Jesus as Son of God.

An interesting case in point is the Lord's Prayer or the "Our Father." Even though most Christians would consider this the preeminent Christian prayer, it does not use Trinitarian language since it was prayed by Jesus as a Jew.[39] Yet at the same time, I have heard from Christians who cannot accept the Muslim *Fatiha* prayer because of the absence of Trinitarian language in this prayer. I do not want to argue that Christians should accept the *Fatiha*—even though I think they could do so—but a refusal based on absence of Trinitarian language seems somewhat arbitrary and even disingenuous if it is directed at one religion specifically, especially if the refusal is based on political considerations or on ignorance. Such a refusal also gives a strange asymmetry to interfaith relations between the Abrahamic traditions, since, while Christians are generally fairly confident that they worship one God together with Jews, Jews are often not so sure because of the association of the Trinity with *avoda zara* or "foreign worship."[40] Conversely, Christians

---

38. I have elaborated on some of these aspects a bit more in "God(s) of Abraham," 28–31. For more on *tahrif*, see the discussion in chapter 2.

39. Crossan, *Greatest Prayer*.

40. See Goshen-Gottstein, "God between Christians and Jews" and Neusner, "Do Monotheist Religions Worship?"

often use the qur'anic denial of divine sonship as an argument against saying that they worship one God together, while Muslims usually state, on the basis of the same Qur'an, that they worship one God together with Jews and Christians, as we have seen at the beginning of this chapter.

So it seems that there are too many asymmetries and misunderstandings to make a dialogue about God fruitful. And yet, the history of Christian-Muslim relationships teaches us that better mutual understanding can be possible as long as the goal of the conversation is not conversion or common ground. If the goal of such a theological conversation is to improve the quality of our understanding of the differences between us, it might lead to a better understanding of the limits of what each of us knows separately about God. Christians should be aware that they know more how God is not than how God is, even though they know God as threefold in relation.[41] It might be that an awareness of our common learned ignorance helps us to find better language that stimulates God-seeking between traditions rather than erecting boundaries.[42]

## Do We Worship the Same God?

In the fall of 2012, two books were published with almost the same title: Do We Worship the Same God?[43] The contents of these two books make clear that the answer to this question is not as easy as many people may be inclined to think. Since both books contain substantial dialogue between Jewish, Christian, and Muslim authors, they are products of a conciliatory rather than confrontational style of encounter between the three religions. And yet, as I have made clear in the beginning of this chapter, I do not think that "do we worship the same God?" is a particularly helpful question, since it invites us to make sometimes superficial comparisons in an endeavor to find common ground. Just like the "common word" verse in the Qur'an (discussed in the first section above), an effort to find common ground may

---

41. This is not the place to elaborate on Trinitarian theology, but the fact that both St. Augustine and St. Anselm talk about the threeness in God as a *tres nescio quid* ("three I don't know what") indicates that the usual talk of three "persons" in God tends to be misleading, as both Karl Rahner and Karl Barth have observed, and that relationality, not individuality, is essential for understanding Trinitarian language. See Marmion and Van Nieuwenhove, *Introduction to the Trinity*.

42. See Heft et al., eds., *Learned Ignorance*.

43. Volf, ed., *Do We Worship the Same God?* and Neusner et al., *Do Jews, Christians, & Muslims Worship the Same God?*

hinder true encounter between Christianity and Islam if it suggests that in the end we all worship the same God in different manners. As Thomas Aquinas reminds us, talking about "the same" suggests that we know what we are talking about, while in fact we do not know how God is, rather we know how God is not. Therefore, he insists on God's simpleness, implying that basic characteristics of our language do not apply when we try to talk about the God who is Creator of heaven and earth.

In this respect, the "Common Word process" and the two books discussed here remind us that it is not easy to find simple answers. The history of apologetic and polemical literature on God between Muslims and Christians teaches us the same lesson: the goal of these theological discussions cannot be to find common ground or a basic sameness. The goal of these discussions is to deepen our awareness that we do not know Whom we are talking about, and yet we need to keep on trying. In talking about the differences between us we will be led toward the greater truth that God will show us in the end, as the Qur'an says (Q 5:48).

## A Word in Our Time

A contemporary discussion of God in the context of Christian-Muslim dialogue will profit from a fresh reading of the document that proved to be a landmark in Christian-Muslim relations, the *Declaration on the Relation of the Church to Non-Christian Religions, Nostra aetate*, proclaimed by Pope Paul VI at the Second Vatican Council in October 1965. Even though this document is over fifty years old, it contains texts about the relation between Christians and Muslims that have not yet been fully recovered, let alone put into practice.[44] The start of the third section of *Nostra aetate* is very clear about the question whether Muslims worship the One God: "The Church also regards with esteem the Muslims. They adore the one God, who is living and subsisting in himself, merciful and all-powerful, the Creator of heaven and earth, who has spoken to humans; they strive to submit wholeheartedly even to His inscrutable decrees, just as Abraham, with whom the faith of Islam is gladly linked, submitted to God."[45]

One year earlier, the Council gave a similar description in section 16 of the *Dogmatic Constitution on the Church, Lumen gentium*, namely: "The

44. See Valkenberg and Cirelli, eds., *Nostra Aetate*; also D'Costa, *Vatican II*.

45. Second Vatican Council, *Nostra aetate*, 3 (para. 1), in Valkenberg and Cirelli, eds., *Nostra Aetate*, xx.

plan of salvation also includes those who acknowledge the Creator, in the first place among them the Muslims who, professing to hold the faith of Abraham, along with us adore the one and merciful God, who on the last day will judge humankind."[46] This text is not only unambiguous about the fact that Christians and Muslims do indeed together adore the one God—the Latin text says *nobiscum Deum adorant unicum*—but it also gives the basic tenets that Muslims and Christians share about this God: He is the Creator of heaven and earth; He has communicated with human beings, specifically Abraham; and He will judge humankind on the last day. This text echoes what the Qur'an says about believing in one God and the last judgment, and acting righteously, as reasons for human beings to be hopeful about their reward with God.[47] It adds that this faith is modeled after the faith of Abraham, and it seems to recognize—in a somewhat circumspect way—the Abrahamic claim that the religion of Islam represents.[48] In summary, the text indicates three ways of approaching God that might guide Muslims and Christians in their future dialogues about God: God as creator of heaven and earth; God as inspiring and challenging the faith of Abraham and his heritage; God as passing final judgment over our human existence.

46. Second Vatican Council, *Lumen gentium*, 16.

47. *Lumen gentium* does not explicitly mention "acting righteously" in the passage about the Muslims, but it mentions this element later in the same section 16.

48. See Valkenberg, "*Nostra Aetate*," 24. On the influence of Louis Massignon on this text, see Krokus, *Theology of Louis Massignon*.

## 2

# The Paraclete and the Integrity of Scripture

## Sandra Toenies Keating

HISTORICALLY, ONE OF THE most contentious disagreements between
Muslims and Christians has been whether Jesus predicted Muhammad. The
followers of Muhammad saw him as the final messenger in a long line of
messengers, like Moses and Jesus, sent from God, the Seal of the Prophets
(*Khatim al-Nabiyin*), who came to confirm and correct errors in the scriptural interpretation of the "People of the Book" (e.g., Q 3:50; 5:46; 4:171).
Yet, for Christians this did not seem likely or even possible. Orthodox
Christians had held that Jesus Christ is the culmination of God's plan of
salvation and that no further revelation to humanity is necessary. Further,
by the seventh century, the process of canonization of the scriptures was
widely recognized as complete,[1] making the notion that serious errors had
crept into scripture and its authoritative interpretation so that God needed
to send a messenger or prophet to correct them appear ludicrous. For the
young Muslim community, however, it was of prime importance that conti-
nuity between the prophets of old and Muhammad be established in order
to affirm the legitimacy of the revelations to the *ummi* messenger.[2]

---

1. The formation of the biblical canon is an extremely complex and an ongoing debate among scholars; nonetheless, it is widely agreed that by the end of the fourth century
Christian churches, both east and west, identified a common canon to which nothing
could be added or changed. See for example, Hahneman, "The Muratorian Fragment and
the Origins of the New Testament Canon."

2. *Ummi* is an epithet given to Muhammad in the Qur'an, especially in 62:2, which
likely means "unscriptured" but has traditionally been understood as "unlettered."

## Who Is the Paraclete?

The concern to reinforce Muhammad's legitimacy as an anticipated prophet in the well-established line of Jewish and Christian figures appears in his own lifetime. Already in the Qur'an, one finds the assertion that the followers of Jesus were told to expect another, who has now come in the person of Muhammad. Q 61:7 states that:

> And [remember] when Jesus, the son of Mary, said, "O children of Israel, indeed I am the messenger (*rasul*) of Allah to you, confirming what came before me in the Torah and bringing good tidings of a messenger to come after me, whose name is Ahmad." But when he came to them with clear proofs, they said, "This is obvious sorcery."[3]

This "reminder" can be taken as an indication that the claim was being met with general, though perhaps not systematic, resistance. Within a century after Muhammad's death, the assertion was a well-known point of tension and Muslim scholars worked to understand how this prophetic expectation noted in the Qur'an could be true. One might conjecture that as Muslims and Christians engaged in more intense conversations about these predictions and more educated Christians joined the new movement, it became apparent that the Gospels did not include any explicit reference to a prophet or messenger after Jesus. Nonetheless, at some point, Muslims came to the conclusion that verses in the Gospel of John concerning Jesus' sending of the Paraclete were in fact remnants of the prediction of another messenger (14:16; 15:26; and 16:7).

The exact origin of the identification between Muhammad and the Paraclete remains unclear, although references are found in both Muslim and Christian sources. One of the earliest Muslim accounts is found in the *Sirat Rasul Allah*, in which Ibn Ishaq (d. before 770) explains that one finds in the Gospel of John these words of Jesus:

> But the word that is in the law [*al-namus*] must be fulfilled, 'They hate me without a cause' (i.e. without reason). But when the Comforter [*al-munhamanna*] has come whom God will send to you from the Lord's presence, and the spirit of truth [*al-qist*][4] which

---

3. All translations of the Qur'an are my own, unless otherwise noted.

4. A better translation is "spirit of justice." Some later manuscripts correct this as *quds* ("holy"), although Ibn Hisham's version is consistent with the Christian Palestinian Aramaic (CPA), *rwh' d-qwsht*. The CPA version is likely the biblical source for his text.

will have gone forth from the Lord's presence he (shall bear) witness of me and ye also, because ye have been with me from the beginning . . . .[5]

The editor of the *Sirat*, Ibn Hisham (d. 833), adds that "The Munahhemana [sic] (God bless and preserve him!) in Syriac is Muhammad; in Greek he is the paraclete [*al-baraqlitis*]."[6]

Christians countered with their own explanations and one finds in several recensions in the legend about a monk named Bahira circulating at this time references to a Jew named Ka'b the Scribe, who misled the followers of Muhammad to believe "and follow this tradition that Muhammad is the Paraclete."[7] To date, the earliest extant Christian reference to the controversy is found in the "Correspondence of Leo III and 'Umar II," which has been credibly established as having its origin at least as early as the middle of the eighth century.[8] In one of the most complete manuscripts of the "Correspondence," Leo explains to 'Umar that the Paraclete was sent by

See Anthony, "Muhammad, Menahem, and the Paraclete," 260n22. Wüstenfeld notes the three manuscripts that substitute *quds* for *qist*. See Wüstenfeld and Band, eds., *Das Leben Muhammed's nach Muhammed Ibn Ishak bearbeitet von Abd el-Malik Ibn Hischam*, 48.

5. Ibn Ishaq, *Life of Muhammad*, 104 (Arabic edition: Wüstenfeld and Band, 150).

6. Ibid. Ibn Ishaq's unusual translation of the Greek *parakletos* as *munhamanna* has long puzzled scholars. Recently, however, it has been convincingly argued that a CPA rendering of the passage was the source of Ibn Ishaq's version. For an excellent exposition of the hypothesis, see Anthony, "Muhammad, Menahem," 255–78. If Anthony's suggestion is correct, the strong Jewish apocalyptic expectations of late antique Palestine form the context within which Muhammad's followers came to identify him as the Comforter, the Messiah called Menahem. Christians consequently challenged any notion that a further Messiah was expected, emphasizing that the two Paracletes of 1 John 2:1 and John 14:16–19 were in fact Jesus Christ and the Spirit of Truth through a shift in translation of proof texts. See especially Anthony, "Muhammad, Menahem," 261–63, 270–73.

7. Roggema, *Legend of Sergius Bahira*, 269; see also ibid., 303, 335, 391. The basic outline of the Bahira story is that at the age of twelve, Muhammad was recognized by a Christian monk as the noble prophet about whom Jesus prophesied. Christians and Muslims have had radically different interpretations of this monk—Christians often arguing that he was a Nestorian charlatan who intended to deceive; Muslims claiming that his recognition of Muhammad's true identity is proof of the authenticity of the latter's prophethood. Variations of the story are ubiquitous, and usually reflect the interest of the source, making it difficult to determine the truth of the initial event. Roggema's book is an outstanding study of the extant material.

8. Hoyland, "Correspondence of Leo III (717–41) and 'Umar II (717–20)." Cecilia Palombo argues it is slightly later, but maintains that it represents one of the earliest texts of Christian apologetic literature written in Arabic. See her article, "'Correspondence' of Leo III." See also Kim, "Arabic Letters."

Jesus to console those whom he had left behind and support them in their mission to spread the gospel. Leo writes: "Paraclete thus signifies 'consoler,' while Muhammad means 'to give thanks,' or 'to render grace,' a meaning which has no connection whatever with the word Paraclete."[9] He goes on to say that it is the worst kind of blasphemy to replace the Holy Spirit with someone who is ignorant of the Holy Scriptures. This indicates that the explanation of Muhammad's identification with the Paraclete given by Ibn Hisham in the *Sirat* was already current much earlier and had perhaps already become a central point of contention early in the century following Muhammad's death. The topic is noted in several other texts, among which are the Arabic disputation between the Caliph al-Mahdi with the Patriarch Timothy I that took place around 781[10] and in the Syriac *'Elta d-mawteh d-Muhammad* ("The affair of the death of Muhammad")[11] associated with the Bahira legends, all of which can be dated to the eighth or early-ninth century, and reflect the concern of Christians to counter the Muslim claim that Muhammad was predicted in the Bible.

In the mid-ninth century, 'Ali ibn Rabban al-Tabari (c. 780–c. 860), who converted from East-Syrian Christianity to Islam late in life, produced two significant apologetic works outlining his criticisms of Christianity. In the later work, *Kitab al-din wa-l-dawla*, "The Book of Religion and Empire" (composed c. 855), al-Tabari devotes his tenth chapter to "The Prophecy of Christ about the Prophet (may God bless them and give them peace)."[12] He begins the section with an explanation of the verses in John's Gospel concerning the Paraclete and lays out four arguments supporting the notion that this is a prediction of Muhammad. First, al-Tabari claims that the meaning of the verse, "The Paraclete, the Spirit of truth, whom my Father will send in my name will teach you all things" (John 14:26), is that "all things" includes what was not known before, and since the disciples of Christ have only taught what he taught them, the Paraclete must be one who teaches what was not known before. Thus, the Paraclete is the Prophet Muhammad and the Qur'an is the unknown knowledge.[13] Al-Tabari goes on to interpret John 16:7, 8, 13 and 14:16 in which Christ says "He [the Father] will send

9. Jeffery, "Ghevond's Text," 293.

10. Mingana, *Apology of Timothy*, 169–71; Heimgartner, ed., *Timotheos I*; and Heimgartner, *Einleitung, Übersetzung, und Anmerkungen*, 38–43. See an excerpt in Tieszen, *Textual History*, 50–57.

11. Roggema, "Affair of the Death," 401–2.

12. See an excerpt in Tieszen, *Textual History*, 104–9.

13. Al-Tabari, *Polemical Works*, 424–25.

him [the Paraclete] in my [Christ's] name" as referring to Christ's name-sake, which is Muhammad, since both are mentioned together in the books of the prophets.[14] Further, al-Tabari gives a numerological proof, claiming that the numerical sum of the letters of *faraqlit* equals the total of the letters of "Muhammad son of 'Abd Allah, prophet, guide [*Muhammad bin 'Abd Allah, al-nabi al-hadi*]."[15] Finally, the Paraclete is described as the "Spirit of truth" (John 16:17), and according to the disciple John, "every spirit that does not believe that Christ was corporeal is not from God" (1 John 4:2–3). Muhammad, following the Qur'an, knew that Christ was God's spirit that he cast into Mary (Q 4:171), and also knew that Christ was corporeal.[16] The implication is that the Paraclete, the Spirit of truth, must be corporeal, and this supports the Muslim claim that the Paraclete is Muhammad. But, in spite of the current popularity of al-Tabari's arguments, his writings were apparently not cited by Muslim writers until the eleventh century.[17]

Another Muslim commentator on the Bible, Ibn Qutayba (828–889), was a much more popular source for his contemporaries. He includes references to Jesus' prediction of Muhammad in his well-known *A'lam* (or *Dala'il) al-nubuwwa* ("Proofs of Prophethood"), citing similar arguments as his predecessors.[18] Although Ibn Qutayba includes nearly all of the same biblical passages as al-Tabari, the discrepancies in translation of those texts into Arabic point to different traditions, which may be a clue as to the source of original identification of the Paraclete with Muhammad. Ibn Qutayba's list of biblical passages referring to the coming of another messenger from God are drawn almost entirely from the Prophet Isaiah and the Gospel of John, and include those most commonly cited in the following centuries.[19]

14. Ibid. This argument is somewhat obscure since it is not clear which "books of the prophets" are meant here. It is noteworthy that many of the verses cited by Ibn Qutayba (discussed below) from the Prophet Isaiah and the Psalms might be interpreted to refer to two different people. Such grammatical parsing was common among Christians who sought to use Old Testament passages in typological references to the Holy Trinity and Jesus Christ.

15. Ibid., 426–27.

16. Ibid.

17. Schmidtke, "Muslim Reception," 250–51. A cursory search on the Internet reveals al-Tabari as the most commonly cited ancient source for contemporary Muslim defenses of Jesus' prediction of Muhammad, while Ibn Qutayba remains generally unknown.

18. For an excellent analysis of Ibn Qutayba's use of the Bible, see Schmidtke, especially 251–60.

19. Schmidtke provides a critical edition of the first eight sections of Ibn Qutayba's text with references to the biblical passages in question in ibid., 254–60.

A proposal one finds in more recent Islamic apologetic to explain the interpretation of the Paraclete draws a connection between the Arabic *ahmad* (following Q 61:7) and the Greek *parakletos*. "According to this argument, the Greek *parakletos* ('comforter/advocate') was either misread or misunderstood as *periklutos*—meaning 'renowned', 'far-famed', or even (with a little imagination) 'praised one.'"[20] Although this argument is commonly noted by contemporary Muslims, its first known appearance is in the writings of the seventeenth century Italian professor of Arabic, Fr. Ludovicco Marracci. In his *Refutatio Alcorani*, he opined that the Greek term was misunderstood when alternative vowels were added to the consonantal skeleton of *p.r.k.l.t.s.* There are numerous linguistic and historical arguments against the veracity of this suggestion,[21] and no contemporary scholar has substantiated it, in spite of its widespread appearance on the Internet.

In sum, the search for predictions of Muhammad in the New Testament, prompted by qur'anic references to Jesus' promise of another messenger led to the Muslim identification of the Paraclete with the Arabian prophet. Over time, scholars sought to explain why it was that these references had been misunderstood, occasioning an entire body of apologetic literature that continues to affect relations between Muslims and Christians.

## The Challenge of Tahrif

At the heart of the controversy surrounding the correct identity of the Paraclete is the question of whether Christians should have recognized Muhammad as the one who was predicted by Jesus and attested to in the Bible, and therefore should have accepted him as a legitimate messenger of God. However, very few Christians (or Jews) joined the early followers of the Arabian prophet and most refused to acknowledge him as one of their own. Over the centuries, Muslim thinkers began to develop a more systematic explanation for this setback, and the claim of Q 61:7 became an assumption, explicit or implicit, in all levels of Muslim-Christian encounters. As Christians argued more and more strenuously that Muhammad was not a prophet (most often because he did not perform miracles and came as a conqueror, rather than as a peaceful preacher) and that the only biblical references to one who would "come after" Jesus Christ signified the Holy Spirit and not a human being, the more insistently Muslims asserted that

20. Anthony, "Muhammad, Menahem," 274.

21. Ibid.

Christians were either misinterpreting their scriptures, or had manipulated them in some way. Consequently, an extensive Islamic teaching of *tahrif*, that is, the assumption of alteration of the meaning or text of the scriptures, was developed to explain the impasse.

The doctrine of *tahrif* finds its foundation in qur'anic verses that indicate the Jews, and subsequently Christians, have intentionally or accidentally misinterpreted their scriptures in several ways, ranging from mispronunciation to forgetting passages to actual substitution of words in order to thwart God's perfect revelation.[22] While early on the emphasis appears to be on the misinterpretation of passages, as the doctrine of *tahrif* developed, Muslim thinkers focused on actual substitution of words as the source of the problem. Thus, within the Islamic commentary tradition, some scholars, such as al-Tabari (mentioned above), generally accepted the integrity of the Jewish and Christian scriptures, but argued they had been misunderstood/misinterpreted, while others, such as al-Jahiz (d. 869), 'Abd al-Jabbar, and Ibn Hazm (d. 1063), claimed the Christian scriptures themselves had been manipulated by "deceitful liars," and cannot be relied upon to provide authentic revelation from God.[23] These latter scholars took as their guide Q 2:75–79, which claim that the Book of the Israelites was altered (*yuharrifuna*) after it was understood by some of them. The passage concludes with the admonishment: "Woe to those who write the Book with their own hands, then they say, 'This is from God', so they may sell it for a small price."

Space limitations here do not allow for a complete examination of the complex development of the teaching of *tahrif*, but a few widely held tenets can be identified. First, the Qur'an employs multiple terms to indicate various types of alteration. The terms can be categorized according to two recognizable groups—*tahrif al-ma'ani* (alteration/corruption of the *meaning* of authentic scriptures) and *tahrif al-nass* (alteration/corruption of the actual *text* of the scriptures). A further distinction made within *tahrif al-ma'ani* is that of *ta'wil*, or manipulation of the interpretation of the meaning of the text. Of the six verbs and their derivatives used in the Qur'an to describe the corruption of the scriptures through human interference,[24] the

22. Numerous Qur'an verses allude to alteration, either in meaning or text, of the Jewish and Christian scriptures. Some of the clearest are Q 2:41–42, 140, 146; 3:71; 7:51–53, 162.

23. See for example Neil Robinson's examination of Muslim polemic concerning Jesus in *Christ in Islam and Christianity*, 46–48.

24. These six—*tahrif, tabdil, kitman, labs, layy,* and *nisyan*—are found in many

most serious is *tabdil*, the substitution of true revelation for something else. Whereas some verses suggest that what was given by God was forgotten or misunderstood, *tabdil* is an intentional and deliberate alteration intended to lead sincere followers away from God. Over time, commentators on the Qur'an generally emphasized *tahrif al-ma'ani* or *tahrif al-nass*, depending on their willingness to accept the integrity of the extant Jewish and Christian scriptures.[25]

Second, the impetus for the teaching of *tahrif* can be found in the need to explain the differences between the revelation to Muhammad and what Jews and Christians claimed in their own teachings, but it is only over time that these explanations are developed and expanded. Thus, one might account for later Muslim references to John's Gospel and the attempt to connect Muhammad to the Paraclete with the desire to explain why Christians claim the Qur'an's assertion of Jesus' prediction of the Prophet is false.[26] The debate developed through the centuries, with each side marshaling more precise arguments to support its claim about Muhammad's prophethood.

What is significant here is the qur'anic claim that the revelation to Muhammad is not new, but rather a return to the original teaching that is accessible to all of humanity. Central to the Qur'an's self-understanding is that it is an Arabic reading of the "Preserved Tablet," which God sent down to Muhammad as a "mercy" (*rahm*) and a "reminder" (*dhikr*) to those who would believe. Muhammad was commanded by the Angel to recite what he would be given. The recitation (*qur'an*) would come from the divine source, the Preserved Tablet (Q 85:22). This Preserved Tablet (*Lawh al-Mahfuz*) is

---

verses, along with numerous implicit references to tampering. See for example, Keating, "Revisiting the Charge," especially 211–15.

25. Several significant studies have been done on the later use of *tahrif* by Muslims, e.g., di Matteo, "Il 'tahrif' od alterazione"; Gaudeul and Caspar, "Textes de la tradition musulmane"; Lazarus-Yafeh, *Intertwined Worlds*; Resnick, "Falsification of Scripture"; Lazarus-Yafeh, "Tahrif," 111a; Accad, "Corruption and/or Misinterpretation"; and Reynolds, "On the Qur'anic Accusation."

26. Some contemporary scholarly attempts to argue that *tahrif* is a later invention are misguided in this respect. While it is certainly true that complex presentations of specific instances of corruption are not found until at least a century after Muhammad, the principle that deviations from the messages received by the Prophet indicate some form of tampering and alteration is clearly present throughout the Qur'an. Thus, Gordon Nickel's study of Muqatil ibn Sulayman's (d. 767) early commentary on the Qur'an is correct that the presumption of misinterpretation instead of falsification of the biblical text dominates, but this does not eliminate the fact that more radical interpretations of substitution that become more prevalent are based on a qur'anic foundation. See Nickel, "Early Muslim Accusations of *Tahrif*," and Nickel, *Narratives of Tampering.*

also referred to as the *Umm al-Kitab*, the Mother of the Book (Q 3:7; 43:4) that is preserved and guarded from all corruption (Q 15:9). It is a fixed text, unchanging and reliable, which guarantees God's promise of mercy and justice. Thus, according to the Qur'an, the original revelation inscribed on the Preserved Tablet contains the prediction of another messenger who will be the Seal of the Prophets. If a reference to such a messenger cannot be found in the scriptures of the Jews and Christians, some account must be given of its absence.

As noted already, the stalemate between Muslims and Christians (and Jews) about the integrity of the scriptures cannot be overcome easily. While Christians generally refuted Muslim claims about the Paraclete using traditional exegesis and arguments defending the integrity of the Bible, Muslims dismissed these, arguing that the People of the Book had been misled by their ancestors. In the end, as the Qur'an advises Muhammad's followers to respond: "O unbelievers, I do not worship what you worship, and you do not worship what I worship, and I will not worship what you worship, and you will not worship what I worship. For you is your religion and for me is my religion" (Q 109:1-6). At the final Judgment, God will sort out what is true and false.

The question of *tahrif* continues to be a central theological issue between Muslims and Christians and Jews, even when it is not addressed directly. In recent times it has been the subject of more focused scholarly attention, and one hopes that a clearer understanding of the origins and intent of the teaching will help overcome deeply rooted suspicions among the three religious communities.[27] Until that time, however, the question of the identity of the Paraclete must remain a matter of faith.

## Theological Questions

Over the centuries, the differing interpretations of the identity of the Paraclete have had a deep impact on relations between Muslims and Christians and left many theological debates at an impasse. At the most basic level, if Jesus the Messiah did promise another person who would come after himself and "teach all things," then Muslims can justifiably claim Muhammad is that person. However, if the promise is the incorporeal Spirit of Truth,

---

27. A recent effort in this direction is found in the commendable collection of articles, Güzelmansur, ed., *Das koranische Motiv der Schriftfälschung (tahrif) durch Juden und Christen.*

as Christians maintain, then Muhammad's claim to be another messenger sent from the God of Abraham, Moses, and Jesus is false.[28] Both Muslims and Christians point to their own scriptures for evidence; both argue the other misinterprets those scriptures, or even has corrupted versions of the original text in their possession.[29] Is there a way beyond this conflict?

In the past few decades, many Muslims and Christians have sought to increase understanding and trust between the two communities, and have looked to their own sacred texts for insights into how to address the issue. Reflecting on the workings of the Holy Spirit beyond the church, Christians have emphasized the unity of all human beings and God's activity in the lives of every person. At the Second Vatican Council (1962–1965), the Roman Catholic Church promulgated several authoritative statements intending to offer guidance in this area. *Nostra aetate*, the *Declaration on the Relation of the Church to Non-Christian Religions*, teaches that "the Catholic Church rejects nothing of what is true and holy in these religions. She has a high regard for the manner of life and conduct, the precepts and doctrines which, although differing in many ways from her own teaching, nevertheless often reflect a ray of that truth which enlightens all men."[30] Further, the ancient doctrine articulated in the early centuries of the church that "the seeds of the Word" are present and active in the various religions can provide a way to think about the value of what is good and true in the scriptures and texts of other religious communities.[31] In light of these statements, Roman Catholics must continue to affirm what is good and true in the Qur'an and the teachings of Muhammad, even while rejecting the claim that the Arabian prophet was predicted by Jesus or that the Qur'an corrects or supersedes the Bible. The Holy Spirit continues to draw all of humanity towards the truth of Jesus Christ in ways beyond our own understanding.

---

28. For more on Christian assessments of Muhammad's prophethood, see chapter 3.

29. Recently, a few scholars have returned to an ancient Christian claim that the Qur'an reflects a garbled version of Christian hymnody or homilies. Although some theories, such as that of Christoph Luxenberg, are quite implausible, other more modest suggestions seek to account for the myriad stories, personages, and loan words that have a strong connection with Jewish and Christian extra-biblical writings. See Luxenberg, *Syro-Aramaic Reading*, and the scathing critiques of his thesis by de Blois, "Book Review"; and Böwering, "Recent Research on the Construction of the Qur'an," 77–79. A less skeptical view of Luxenberg's suggestion is offered in Griffith, "Syriacisms," 94–98.

30. Second Vatican Council, *Nostra aetate*, 2.

31. Second Vatican Council, *Ad gentes*, 11; idem, *Lumen gentium*, 17.

Some Muslims, on the other hand, have emphasized those verses of the Qur'an that acknowledge the divinely-willed differences among religious communities and the continued legitimacy of the Jewish and Christian scriptures. One of the more commonly cited verses is from Q 5:48, in which God speaks to Muhammad about Christians who have rejected his message:

> "And we have revealed to you the Book in truth, confirming the Books that have come before it and as a guardian over it. So judge between them by what Allah has revealed, and do not follow their inclinations away from what has come to you of the truth. To each of you We have prescribed a law and a clear way. Had Allah willed, He would have made you a single community, but [He intends] to test you in what He has given you, so vie with one another in good [works]. To Allah you will all return, and He will inform you concerning that over which you used to differ."

Ultimately, the Qur'an and Christian tradition seem, in my opinion, to point the only way forward. The question of the identity of the Paraclete will remain a matter of faith in this life, and both religious communities are commanded by their scriptures to strive towards goodness and holiness. Until the final judgment, at which time God will reveal the fullness of truth, Christians and Muslims must respond to God's test and vie with one another in good works.

## 3

# Christians, Prophethood, and Muhammad

## Mark Beaumont

### Prophecy in Israel and Idolatry

ONE OF THE FUNCTIONS of prophecy in Israel was to challenge apostasy from the worship of Yahweh. Once the monarchy was established under David (fl. c. 1000 BCE), worship of Yahweh was supported by the king. However, Solomon (r. c. 970–931 BCE), David's son, is said to have turned to worshipping the gods of his various foreign wives in his old age (1 Kgs 11:4) and building shrines for their worship (1 Kgs 11:8). After the death of Solomon Israel divided into two nations. Rehoboam (931–913 BCE) continued to lead the Davidic Southern kingdom in the worship of Yahweh in the temple in Jerusalem. However, Jeroboam (r. 931–910) set up two shrines in Bethel and Dan in the Northern kingdom with a gold calf in each, which he proclaimed had rescued Israel from Egypt (1 Kgs 12:28). An unnamed prophet from Rehoboam's kingdom appeared in the Bethel sanctuary when Jeroboam was about to make an offering and announced that the Lord had sent him to declare that one day the altar would be desecrated with the burnt bones of the priests who offered sacrifices there (1 Kgs 13:2). Jeroboam sent his wife to consult Ahijah the prophet concerning the illness of their son Abijah (r. 913–911). The prophet denounced the apostasy of Jeroboam who had made idols from gold (1 Kgs 14:9). He had not stopped Israelites from setting up poles to worship the goddess Asherah and warned that the Lord would remove the people of the Northern kingdom beyond the river Eurphrates (1 Kgs 14:15). According to Iain Provan, "The goddess Asherah was the consort of the Canaanite god Baal, and Asherah poles are

26

wooden objects used in her worship. The golden calves are thus already being associated with the worship of foreign deities that will break out in Israel with a vengeance during the reign of Ahab."[1]

The later Northern king Ahab (r. 874–853 BCE) encouraged the worship of his wife Jezebel's Sidonian gods. He built a temple for Baal and set up a sacred pole for Asherah (1 Kgs 16:31–33). Jezebel started a campaign to annihilate prophets who spoke in the name of Yahweh (I Kgs 18:4). Ahab was challenged by one of them, named Elijah, to bring the prophets of Baal and Asherah to a contest on Mount Carmel on the northern border with Sidon, because Ahab had disobeyed the Lord by turning to Baal (1 Kgs 16: 18–19). Elijah challenged the gathered representatives of the leadership of the Northern kingdom to choose between Baal and Yahweh, and after the failure of the prophets of Baal to bring down fire on the sacrificial bull, Elijah called on Yahweh to prove he was the only God of Israel by burning up the sacrifice (1 Kgs 16:21–38). This He duly did and Elijah led the people in executing the prophets of Baal at the foot of the mountain (1 Kgs 16:40). Ahaziah (r. 853–852 BCE), son of Ahab, sought healing from Baalzebub rather than Yahweh, and Elijah was sent to announce that because of this he would die (2 Kgs 1:2–4). The next king, Joram (r. 852–841 BCE), destroyed an image of Baal his father had set up, but not the golden calves of Jeroboam (2 Kgs 3:2–3). His successor, Jehu (r. 841–814 BCE), destroyed the shrine to Baal with the prophets who served there, but he did not stop the worship of the calves (2 Kgs 10:28–29). Jehoahaz (r. 814–798 BCE), son of Jehu, continued with the worship of the calves and allowed the worship of Asherah (2 Kgs 13:7). Subsequent kings were indicted by the historian for following Jeroboam's religious practices until the downfall of the Northern kingdom in 722 BCE.

The book of Kings does not mention Hosea, whose prophecies were collected in a book that bears his name. But the contents of those messages demonstrate the nature of the prophetic attack on idolatry. Hosea was called to prophesy in the reign of Jeroboam II (r. 783–743 BCE) that the Northern kingdom would be destroyed (Hos 1:1, 4). Israel had forgotten Yahweh and had put on gold and silver, burned incense, and made offerings of grain, wine, and oil to Baal (Hos 2:8, 13). They had cut themselves asking Baal for fertile crops (Hos 7:14). The calves of Jeroboam would be smashed by Yahweh in his anger (Hos 8:6). The people had become as distasteful to Yahweh as Baal Peor to which they were devoted (Hos 9:10), and Yahweh

---

1. Provan, *1 and 2 Kings*, 120.

threatens to wipe them out in war (Hos 13:15–16). John Day points out how these details reflect what is known of Baal worship in Ugaritic texts. "Baal brings the rain, on which the fertility of the land depends, the rain ceasing with his death and returning with his resurrection."[2] The offerings made to Baal in Hosea 2:8 show that the worshippers believe he is responsible for grain, wine and oil. The reference to cutting the body in Hosea 7:14 "as an act of rebellion against Yahweh is fully explicable if this is understood as a mourning ritual for the god Baal."[3]

The Southern kingdom was not immune from idolatry. Manasseh (r. 687–642 BCE) set up altars for Baal and a sacred pole for Asherah "as Ahab king of Israel had done." He also worshipped the stars (2 Kgs 21:3). Worse still, he worshipped Baal, Asherah, and the stars within the Jerusalem temple (2 Kgs 21:4–6). Several unnamed prophets were given the message from the Lord that He would destroy Jerusalem and Judah because they had become as rebellious as Ahab and Israel had been (2 Kgs 21:12–13).

## Muhammad and Idolatry

According to Aisha (d. 678), one of his future wives, Muhammad was meditating in a cave near Mecca when a voice spoke to him and said, "You are God's messenger." Muhammad was terrified; "I considered throwing myself from the top of a mountain," he told Aisha. Later Muhammad reported that the voice had said, "Recite." Muhammad said, "What shall I recite?" Then the voice said, "Recite in the name of your Lord who created you."[4] This probably took place on the twenty-sixth or twenty-seventh night of Ramadan (c. 610), and is the opening of chapter 96 of the Qur'an. Muhammad doubted his sanity and confided in his then wife Khadija (d. 620). She went to her cousin Waraqa ibn Nawfal who knew the Jewish and Christian scriptures. He said of Muhammad, "There has come unto him the greatest *Namus*, who came to Moses aforetime, and lo, he is the prophet of this people."[5] The second message he received is recorded in Q 74:1–7, when he was covered in a cloak. He is called to get up and warn others, to say how great his Lord is, and to be persevering in proclaiming his Lord. The third time he encountered the angel Gabriel, Muhammad is told, "Remember your Lord's Name and be

2. Day, "Hosea and the Baal Cult," 205.

3. Ibid., 213.

4. Ibn Ishaq, *Life of Muhammad*, 106.

5. Ibid., 107.

completely dedicated to Him. Lord of the East and the West there is no God but He. So make Him your protector" (Q 73:8–9).

Muhammad brought a message that attacked the worship of the created. So from the very beginning of Islam the attack on idolatry is joined. Such utter devotion to God the Creator meant attacking whatever other people may choose to worship. In Muhammad's time Arabs called on several divine beings. Three female deities are mentioned by name in Q 53: al-Lat, al-'Uzza, and Manat. The recitation says of them that "God did not give them any authority" (Q 53:22), and goes on to attack those who pray to heavenly beings. "How many angels are there in heaven, but their intervention [on behalf of men and women] is worthless" (Q 53:26).

There are several references in the Qur'an to the widespread belief among Arabs that the high god had offspring, particularly daughters that were worshipped at the sanctuary in Mecca. Muhammad would have witnessed this worship as a child in Mecca, so it is not surprising that the early messages of Muhammad concentrate on this misguided worship. There are several references to this phenomenon in the Meccan period. In Q 37:149–52 Muhammad is instructed to ask the Meccans, "Does your Lord have daughters, while they have sons? Did We create the angels as females as they witness? Are they not merely inventing this when they say, 'God has begotten children.' Such liars they are." Q 25:2–3 points out why the worship of these so-called "daughters of god" is wrong:

> He has sovereignty over the heavens and the earth and has not begotten a son. He has no associate in his rule. He created everything and appointed everything in its exact place. But they have taken, apart from Him, gods that create nothing, and are themselves created, that have no power in themselves to harm or help, and that have no power over death, life, or resurrection.

The message of Q 21:26–29 challenges the Meccans who believed that God had offspring who were worthy of worship:

> They say, "The Most Merciful has begotten children." May He be glorified! No, they are only His honored servants. They do not speak before He speaks and they act by His command. He knows what is before them and what is behind them. They only intercede for those who are approved. They are those who fear Him with deep reverence. If one of them were to say, "I am a god apart from Him," that one We would reward with Hell. Likewise We reward the evildoers.

Therefore, the central message of Muhammad to his Meccan contemporaries was that the Creator is to be worshipped and that they must give up the worship of the deities to whom they had been accustomed to praying and making offerings. If prophecy in Israel was to maintain the worship of the Creator and elector of Israel against apostasy, then the prophecy of Muhammad was to establish for the first time the true worship of the Creator in his Meccan community against the habitual worship of multiple deities.

## Prophecy in Israel and Social Justice

Another task of prophets in Israel was to hold kings accountable for their use of power over those they ruled. When David committed adultery with the wife of one of his army officers, Uriah, and organized that officer's death in battle, the prophet Nathan, who had at one time announced that the Lord was pleased with David and would maintain his descendants on the throne of Israel in perpetuity (1 Sam 7:16), came to David and told him a story of a rich man who rather than take a lamb from his flock required a pet lamb from a poor tenant farmer of his to serve to guests. David became angry with the rich man but Nathan said, "You are that man" (1 Sam 12:7). Nathan told David, because he had taken another man's wife and murdered that man, that the Lord would stir up disruption in David's family that would bring dishonor to him (1 Sam 12:10–12).

Elijah not only brought messages to Ahab about idolatry, but he also challenged Ahab's unjust seizure of a neighbor's vineyard, after the owner, Naboth, refused to sell it to Ahab. Jezebel had instructed the leaders of Naboth's community to have him executed on the trumped-up charge that he had cursed God and the king (1 Kgs 21:10–14). Elijah was sent to Ahab to tell him that since he had murdered Naboth, he would be put to death on the very spot where Naboth was killed (1 Kgs 21:19).

Amos, the first prophet to have his messages collected in a book, was especially concerned to warn the powerful to change their unjust behavior towards those they ruled. He mentions that the Lord gave him messages two years before an earthquake, which happened in 760 BCE during the reigns of Uzziah (r. 781–740 BCE) of the Southern kingdom of Judah and Jereboam II (r. 783–743 BCE) of the Northern kingdom of Israel (Amos 1:1). He lists several unjust practices for which the Lord will punish Israel. They sell the poor into slavery for the price of a pair of sandals (Amos 2:6), a father and son sleep with the same woman who is helpless to assert her rights (Amos 2:7), they keep clothes given as security for a loan by poor borrowers who should have had the clothes returned at the end of the day (Amos 2:8), in the shrine they indulge in wine bought with the money of the poor (Amos 2:8), and encourage Nazirites to renounce their vows to abstain from alcohol by joining them in their drinking sessions (Amos 2:12). Amos picks out the wives of the rich landowners for special criticism. Comparing them to cows of Bashan, he pictures them asking their husbands to bring them drinks while abusing the poor (Amos 4:1). He threatens them with being removed from the land with hooks in their flesh (Amos 4:2). These wealthy people have taxed the poor heavily and have used the proceeds to build lavish houses (Amos 5:11). They know how to bribe judges so that the poor are not heard in court (Amos 5:12). They come to worship the Lord but He has had enough of their offerings based on corruption (Amos 6:21–24). They cannot wait for religious festivals to end to make money from false scales and adulterated grain (Amos 8:5–6). The Lord announces that He will destroy them, though a tiny remnant will remain (Amos 9:8). James Nogalski sums up the message of Amos: "God expects justice and righteousness to be the pillars that orient behavior for the faithful."[6]

## Muhammad and Social Justice

Muhammad preached against the rich Meccans who exploited the poor. In Q 107:1–2 he is reminded that, "The person who rebuffs the orphan and who does not encourage the feeding of the poor" is the very one who does not believe that he will meet God on the Day of Judgment. Q 104:1–6 is a message to such a person who thinks that hoarding wealth will last for eternity. Rather the opposite is true, for his wealth will perish in the Fire. Muhammad was himself an orphan who was protected by his uncle, and Q 93:6, 9–10 is a reminder to him to look out for orphans and commend that they be cared for. "Did your Lord not find you an orphan and give you shelter? So do not crush an orphan, and do not drive away the person who asks for your aid." Therefore, the people who will be granted life in the Garden are those who give of their wealth to those who ask for help and to those who are destitute (Q 70:24–25, 35).

---

6. Nogalski, *Book of the Twelve*, 265.

Corrupt Meccan trading practices are condemned in Q 83:1–6:

> Woe to those who give less than they should! When they buy goods
> from people they expect the complete amount, but when they sell
> goods by weight to people they reduce the correct amount. Do
> they not consider that they will be raised up on a dreadful day, a
> day when people will stand before the Lord of the Worlds?

The wealthy are accused of ill-gotten gains at the expense of the poor. Meccans are also judged for treating newborn girls as disposable in Q 16:58–59.

> When one of them is given news of the birth of a girl his face
> becomes dark for he is angry. He hides from the community be-
> cause of the bad news he received. Will he keep her despite the
> shame or bury her in the ground? Such evil decisions they make!

Therefore, the function of prophets is to hold leaders accountable for their rule. Muhammad was very much in the tradition of the Israelite prophets in this regard.

## Prophecy in the Early Christian Communities

The earliest Christian records contain references to prophetic activity. In the first letter written by Paul to the Thessalonians (c. 50), he advises this church that he founded several years previously not to stop the work of God's Spirit by ignoring messages given in the meetings by prophets. This cryptic comment is given fuller explanation a few years later in Paul's first letter to the Christians in Corinth, who were evidently familiar with hearing the word of the Lord through prophets. Paul advocates the prophetic gift as highly beneficial to the church. He urges them to be keen to prophesy (1 Cor 14:39), but he recognizes that not everyone is a prophet (1 Cor 12:29), because God's Spirit chooses to give the gift of prophecy to those he wills (1 Cor 12:11). Gordon Fee defines prophecy in this context as "Spontaneous Spirit-inspired intelligible messages, orally delivered in the gathered assembly, intended for the edification or encouragement of the people."[7]

The Spirit gives other speaking gifts to the church. There are apostles and teachers (1 Cor 12:29). Teachers seem to be those who pass on the content of scripture and comment on it. Apostles are those who have seen the risen Jesus and have been commissioned to witness to him (1 Cor 15:5–8). In another letter of Paul to the Christians in Galatia (c. 50) he introduces

7. Fee, *First Epistle to the Corinthians*, 660.

himself as having been chosen to be an apostle by Jesus Christ and by God the Father who had raised Jesus from the dead (Gal 1:1). In a letter written to Christians in Rome (c. 58), a city Paul had not visited, he said he had been called to be an apostle of Jesus, and thought of himself as Jesus' servant (Rom 1:1), which "expresses the total belongingness, total allegiance, corresponding to the total ownership and authority"[8] of Jesus as Paul's Lord. Testifying to the lordship of Jesus is the mark of a genuine apostle or prophet. In 1 Corinthians 12:1–3, Paul outlines how the Christians can know that someone is speaking by the inspiration of God's Spirit. The Spirit of God would never lead a speaker to dishonor Jesus, but would lead to Jesus being proclaimed as Lord. Anthony Thiselton points out that Paul has already reminded the Corinthian Christians (1 Cor 6:20) that they have been bought with a price "in order to *belong* to Jesus."[9]

This understanding of prophecy is found in the Revelation of John written in a period of severe persecution (c. 90). John sends messages to seven churches in Asia Minor on behalf of the risen Jesus who communicated with him via an angel (Rev 1:1). John wants them to read his prophecy and obey it (Rev 1:3). "Within the congregations prophets are active . . . but there can be false prophets alongside the true."[10] The false prophet in the church at Thyatira has enticed others into immorality and idolatry (Rev 2:20). The church at Ephesus is commended by John for resisting people who said they were apostles but turned out to be impostors (Rev 2:2). This concern with distinguishing true from false speech is found in the first letter of John probably written in the same context as the Revelation of John to churches in Asia Minor. Some have left John's group because they could not affirm that Jesus was the word of God who became human and shed his blood for the forgiveness of sins (1 John 1:1, 7; 2:22–23). He encourages his readers to test prophecies they hear by what is said about Jesus (1 John 4:1–3). Urban von Wahlde indicates that in arguing that, "Every spirit that confesses Jesus (to be) the Christ, come in the flesh, is of God" John thinks of prophecy in a similar way to Paul. "There is a parallel here with 1 Corinthians 12:3."[11]

---

8. Cranfield, *Romans*, 2.

9. Thiselton, *1 Corinthians*, 195.

10. Marshall, *New Testament Theology*, 564.

11. Von Wahlde, *Gospel and Letters of John*, 149.

## Muhammad as Apostle and Prophet to the People of the Book

Muhammad was summoned to speak to the People of the Book who were either Jews or Christians, and the context of his messages shows which group he was addressing. While some of these messages were from the earlier Meccan period, the challenges to Jews and Christians intensified after Muhammad emigrated from Mecca to Medina, after being invited to settle there by Medinan leaders who accepted that he was the apostle of God and were willing to submit to Islam.

In and around Medina there were three Jewish tribes, according to Ibn Ishaq, who initially agreed to accept the leadership of Muhammad without submitting to Islam, but who then reneged on that agreement. The first tribe to "break their agreement with the apostle" were the Banu Qaynuqaʿ who were part of the population in Medina. The apostle "besieged them until they surrendered unconditionally" but he did not punish them.[12] A second Jewish tribe, the Banu al-Nadir, beyond Medina, were asked to contribute to Muhammad's cause, but plotted to assassinate him. On being defeated, they asked Muhammad to let them go into exile carrying any of their property they could on camels and he agreed.[13] A third Jewish tribe, the Banu Qurayza, another Jewish section of the Medinan population, were attacked for insulting the apostle, and not committing their men to defending Medina against the Meccans. After twenty-five days of siege, Muhammad appointed Saʿd ibn Muʿadh to decide what to do with them. He said, "I give judgement that the men should be killed, the property divided, and the women and children taken as captives," to which Muhammad replied, "You have given the judgement of Allah above the seven heavens."[14] After the surrender of the Banu Qurayzaʿ, "the apostle went out to the market of Medina and dug trenches in it. Then he sent for them and struck off their heads in those trenches . . . There were 600 or 700 in all, though some put the figure as high as 800 or 900."[15] Ibn Ishaq says that this story is mentioned in Q 33. He is probably referring to 33:26–27: "Those People of the Book who supported the unbelievers God brought down from their fortifications and put terror in their hearts. You killed some of them and took

---

12. Ibn Ishaq, *Life of Muhammad*, 363.
13. Ibid., 437.
14. Ibid., 464.
15. Ibid.

others captive. He gave you their land, their houses, and their possessions, and a land which you had not traversed." It seems there was an escalation of retribution for Jewish tribes that did not fully support Muhammad's leadership, from forgiveness, to exile, and finally death for the males and captivity for their families.

Ibn Ishaq does not say much about Christians in Mecca apart from Khadija's uncle and a Christian slave named Jabr who Muhammad used to talk to at a market stall. This led to people alleging that "the one who teaches Muhammad most of what he brings is Jabr the Christian." Ibn Ishaq then says that Q 16:103—"We know that they say that a human being teaches him"—was revealed to refute this accusation.[16] The most interesting story reported by Ibn Ishaq concerning Muhammad's relations with Christians is the deputation of twenty Christians to see Muhammad in Mecca, after he had conquered the town. Ibn Ishaq is not sure whether they came from Ethiopia or Najran, but he says that they accepted the prophethood of Muhammad once they met him. "The apostle invited them to come to God and read the Qur'an to them. When they heard the Qur'an their eyes flowed with tears, and they accepted God's call, believed in him, and declared the truth. They recognized in him the things that had been said of him in their scriptures."[17] Meccans are once again portrayed as ridiculing connections between Christians and Muhammad because they mocked these twenty converts to Muhammad's message for giving up their faith so easily. However, the new followers of Muhammad replied that they "had not been remiss in seeking what is best."[18]

The significance of this story lies in the numbers involved. Waraqa, the cousin of Khadija, was a solitary individual who had recognized that Muhammad was predicted in the Bible, but now a group of twenty follows in his steps. This incremental acceptance of Muhammad by professing Christians is proof for Ibn Ishaq that the prophethood of Muhammad had been foretold in the scriptures of the Christians, and implies that any Christians who paid close attention to the Bible would agree that Muhammad was indeed sent by God, not only to the Arabic speaking tribes of Arabia, but also to Syriac and Ethiopic speakers, and that now was the time to acknowledge this new work of God in the history of the world. Moreover, Ibn Ishaq records the view that this deputation is referred to in the

16. Ibid., 180.

17. Ibid., 179.

18. Ibid.

Qur'an where those who had received "the book," on hearing the revelation brought by Muhammad, proclaimed, "We believe in it, since it is the truth from our Lord. In fact, we have been Muslims before this" (Q 28:52–53) and where devout Christians listened to the revelation brought by the Messenger of God and "their eyes flowed with tears from realizing the truth, saying 'we believe; include us among the witnesses'" (Q 5:82–83). Ibn Ishaq seeks to anchor this significant event in the history of the revelation of the Qur'an to show that God wills that Christians acknowledge that Muhammad was sent by Him to lead Christians to an authentic faith and practice.

Whether this story represents typical Christian responses to Muhammad is not possible to discern from Ibn Ishaq, given that he does not portray Muhammad ruling any Christian groups directly in the way that he ruled Jewish clans. Christians appear to be on the periphery of Muhammad's domain. In the light of what is known about Christianity in the Arabian Peninsula it is hardly credible that many of them would have been willing to affirm someone who claimed to speak for the Creator while regarding Jesus as merely His messenger. Tariq Ramadan thinks that Muhammad's attitude to the Najran Christians was "based on knowledge, sincerity and humility,"[19] but his knowledge of Christianity was rather limited according to the evidence in the Qur'an.

The message to Christians in the Qur'an tends to be critical, although there are some appreciative comments. Q 57:27–28 say that most of the followers of Jesus failed to be merciful and compassionate as God had intended them to be, though a minority who believed in God would receive a reward. Christians are urged to fear God and believe in His messenger. Q 5:82–83 single out Christians from Jews and polytheists as closer to Muslims because among them there are scholars and monks who are not proud and who will be reduced to tears when they hear the message of Muhammad, and who will immediately submit to the truth that he brings. Q 5:116 implies that there were followers of Jesus who worshipped Jesus and Mary as gods alongside God, and this seems to be the basis for Q 4:171 and Q 5:73 that call on Christians to give up the concept of "threeness" and to testify that God is one and that He does not have a son. Q 5:116 portrays Jesus as denying before God that he had called on people to worship him and his mother, and that he only urged them to worship his Lord. Q 5:75–77 urge those who persist in seeing Jesus as more than a messenger, as one with power to benefit them, to draw back from excessive claims to avoid

19. Ramadan, *Messenger*, 117.

a painful outcome on the Day of Judgment. Q 4:157–159 challenge Christians to admit that their story of Jesus dying on the cross is a fabrication, and to confess that God exalted him. The implication of this denial of the crucifixion appears to be that God would never have allowed his messenger to be debased through crucifixion. Christians need to honor Jesus rather than defame him.

How might Christians evaluate these messages addressed to them? From the standpoint of the apostolic writings, John's test that prophets should affirm that Jesus is the Word of God who became human and who died for the forgiveness of sins appears to have failed on both counts. They do not pass Paul's test that prophets honor Jesus as Lord, since the Lordship of Jesus is emphatically denied even by Jesus himself. Christians have often protested that their Trinitarian convictions are not represented in these verses that critique "threeness," and that their view of the sonship of Jesus is not presented adequately in them.

Some Muslims have acknowledged these realities. Farid Esack accepts that the term 'threeness' may have been imposed on Christians but has been rejected by them.[20] "Most Christians insist that the doctrine of the Trinity is not the same as Tritheism, the worship of three gods."[21] Mahmoud Ayoub has noted that the Qur'an does not use the term *walad*, meaning physical offspring, specifically to refer to Jesus. "The Qur'an nowhere accuses Christians of calling Jesus the *walad* offspring of God."[22] Ayoub argues that the term *ibn*, used once in the Qur'an, "may be understood metaphorically to mean 'son' through a relationship of love or adoption."[23] Ayoub also asks his fellow Muslims to reconsider the apparent denial of the crucifixion in Q 4:157–158. "The Qur'an is not speaking here about a man, righteous and wronged though he may be, but about the Word of God who was sent to earth and who returned to God. Thus the denial of the killing of Jesus is a denial of the power of human beings to vanquish and destroy the divine Word, which is forever victorious."[24] Nevertheless, the notion that Jesus shed his blood for the sins of others appears to be a stretch too far. Mona Siddiqui is willing to accept that Jesus was crucified but not that he died to atone for sin. "Even if Muslims came to believe that Jesus did die on the

20. Esack, *Qur'an, Liberation & Pluralism*, 152–53.

21. Ibid., 177.

22. Ayoub, "Jesus the Son of God," 118.

23. Ibid.

24. Ayoub, "Toward an Islamic Christology II," 176.

cross before he was raised, in the Qur'anic frame of references this death has no atoning significance and would not be seen as the decisive event in the redemption plan for humankind."[25]

## Christian Assessments of the Prophethood of Muhammad

What kind of prophecy do Christians perceive in the Qur'an? Kenneth Cragg has thought more deeply about this question than any other Christian in recent times. In *Muhammad and the Christian, A Question of Response* he urges his fellow Christians to take "the Qur'an in positive terms, both in its time and through the centuries as effectively revelatory."[26] He outlines the nature of this effective revelation:

> We receive in the Qur'an a powerful and telling reinforcement of Christian conviction as to the reality and rule of God, the divine creation, the earth tenancy and investiture of man, the divine liability about Him, the intelligible trust of His signs, the interacting claims of worship and dominion, the solemn joy of sexuality, and the awe of our personal being as lived "in the light of His countenance." Whatever the reservations we still have to make, and allowing the fact that predicates about God differ within their agreements, we are not thereby deprived of a community of belief with the people of the Qur'an which is authentic in its content and urgent in its significance.[27]

In a subsequent study of the prophethood of Muhammad, Cragg acknowledges that Muhammad prophesied like the Hebrew prophets. They all spoke for the Creator of humanity and called on their hearers to submit to Him. But Muhammad became a head of state whereas the Hebrew prophets never became kings. "Hebrew prophets knew exile not Hijra. They moved in the courts of political power but did not usurp them."[28] This move to power rather than suffering means that the prophetic work of Muhammad has to be fulfilled in another way by another kind of prophet. "Jesus

---

25. Siddiqui, *Christians, Muslims, and Jesus,* 231.

26. Cragg, *Muhammad and the Christian,* 94–95.

27. Ibid., 118.

28. Cragg, *Weight in the Word,* 20.

crucified had realized in an inclusive way what the precedents of suffering prophethood had foreshown."[29]

This assessment is echoed by Chawkat Moucarry who believes that Muhammad thought he was following prophets named in the Bible, and preached the oneness of God in his polytheistic Arab context. "The Qur'an presents a coherent body of beliefs about God, creation, revelation, humankind, the general resurrection and the Day of judgment, to mention only the major themes . . . . God's attributes in Islam broadly correspond to what we find in the Bible."[30] However, the Qur'an "fails to point to God as the *Savior*, the God who achieved our salvation through the death and resurrection of Jesus Christ . . . . Because the Qur'an does not know God in this way, it fails to recognize the very nature of Jesus' mission."[31] Moucarry calls Muhammad the Prophet of Islam because he thinks that the prophetic activity of Muhammad was not that of the Biblical prophets.[32]

Martin Bauschke understands Islam as a valid mode of revelation. "God wanted both religions as authentic ways to salvation. God revealed himself to both, Jesus and Muhammad!"[33] It follows that the Bible and the Qur'an are both the word of God. "If Christianity and Islam are equal ways to God, then Jesus and Muhammad shall become the two younger brothers of Moses, and the Bible and the Qur'an shall become the second and third testaments of God, added to the first testament, the Torah."[34] He wants Christians to come to recognize Muhammad "as God's Prophet."[35] This would be possible if they came to see "The mission of Jesus and of Muhammad, the revelation of the Word of God as incarnation and as inlibration as being *complementary* . . . Jesus and Muhammad are not doubles, but brothers with similarities and differences."[36] The powerless death of Jesus and the powerful rule of Muhammad are two different modes of God's revelation in different times and situations.

---

29. Ibid., 113.

30. Moucarry, *Faith to Faith*, 257.

31. Ibid.

32. Ibid., 268.

33. Bauschke, "Christian View of Islam," 148.

34. Ibid., 149.

35. Ibid., 152.

36. Ibid. For a wider range of Christian views of Muhammad see Beaumont, "Christian Views of Muhammad."

If we were to evaluate these three approaches to the prophethood of Muhammad, we could begin by pointing out that Bauschke's argument that God willed that some humans received a Christian version of revelation and others a Muslim one was first presented by the Muslim scholar Seyyed Hossein Nasr:

> Was Christ crucified or was he taken alive to Heaven and not crucified as asserted by Islam? Here one faces what seems to be an insurmountable obstacle. One could say that a major cosmic event at the end of the earthly life of Christ could in fact be "seen" and "known" in more than one way, and that it is God's will that Christianity should be given to "see" that end in one way and Islam in another.[37]

The problem with this concession to radical difference in the understanding of the ending of Jesus' life lies in the confidence that Nasr and Bauschke have in their knowledge of the "will" of God. This approach might be taken to anyone who claimed to have had an encounter with God, such as Joseph Smith, who offered the world the Book of Mormon as the word of God. Why should his claim be dismissed as clashing with the Christian and Muslim versions of revelation? A fundamental disparity should not discount the "truth" of an alternative account of divine disclosure in the Nasr/Bauschke scenario. But, in reality, the "will" of God dies the death of a thousand qualifications. There is no alternative to serious scrutiny of claims to reporting the speech of God.

Moucarry's admission that Muhammad brought messages that confirm central teachings of the Bible about the Creator and His relationship to His creation is an example of serious scrutiny of one claim to revelation over against another. Moucarry is reticent to call Muhammad a "Biblical prophet" though he does not explain why. Presumably this is because Muhammad's messages do not completely conform to any of the prophetic examples found in the Bible. However, Muhammad speaks like Elijah or Hosea in condemning idolatry, and shows the same courage to confront the powerful people who promote and uphold the worship of the created rather than the Creator. He is a "Biblical prophet" like them. Muhammad criticizes the same powerful people for ignoring the rights of the poor and disadvantaged just as Amos takes the powerful idolaters to task for treading on the needy to maintain their self-indulgent lifestyle. Muhammad is a "Biblical prophet" like Amos.

37. Nasr, "Comments," 464.

Cragg is more ready to see Muhammad in the way of a Hebrew prophet than Moucarry is. Yet he wishes that Muhammad had stayed as a prophet condemning bad leadership than becoming a leader himself who took to condemning those who followed the message of the Bible. If only Muhammad had been willing to accept exile from Mecca but not rule in Medina, then the prophethood of Muhammad would not have turned into the kingship of Muhammad. He regrets that Muhammad usurped power rather than remaining a critic of the powerful in God's name. For Cragg, prophethood and kingship do not go together, since Hebrew prophets were raised up by God as the conscience of the kings.

Both Moucarry and Cragg lament the absence of the message of salvation through the self-giving of God in Jesus in the messages of Muhammad. If only Muhammad had perceived the truth of the redemption that God provided in the sending of Jesus to reconcile rebellious humanity to Himself. By the criterion of the New Testament documents, Muhammad is not a "Christian prophet." The Matthean, Markan, Lukan, Johannine, and Pauline witness to Jesus is barely heard in the messages that Muhammad brought. Muhammad is a spokesperson for the Creator who holds His human creatures accountable to Him for their attitudes and behavior, but he is not a spokesperson for the Son of the Father who, centuries before Muhammad, revealed the Creator in a new way and shed his blood as a ransom for the wayward children that the Creator loved. Muhammad may have been a prophet like Hosea and Amos, but he was not an apostle like John or Paul.

# 4

# Muslims, Prophethood, and Jesus

## TARIQ RAMADAN

PROPHECY IS FUNDAMENTAL TO the Muslim tradition. It determines not only the nature of the relation God has established with humanity, but also sets forth a singular conception of mankind and of history. Multiple questions surround the very concept of prophecy: the status of the particular human being who is the Prophet, that Prophet's mission on earth, and more broadly speaking, the meaning of the message transmitted and, ultimately, the higher objectives revealed to human beings. There exist, of course, substantial differences between the three monotheistic traditions: the Jewish conception of prophecy can be clearly distinguished from the diverse Christian interpretations (Catholicism, Protestantism, and the Eastern Christian churches). Likewise, the Islamic tradition does not exactly share the Jewish and Christian conceptions even though, in some areas, it hews more closely to the former.

The subject is of central importance, as it offers us access to the essential characteristics of faith and the hope it generates as illuminated by the diversity of mankind's conceptions of God, of Revelation, and of the role of Messengers. It is here, precisely, that we can locate one of the major differences between Christianity and Islam. The respective status of their Revealed Books and their Messengers has been the subject of countless comparative studies and debates between their respective representatives.

As we narrow our focus, we can single out a certain number of mileposts along our analytical route. First we must clarify the meaning of prophecy in Islam: what is it; what does it represent; what does it reveal?

Taking our answer as a starting point, we can then turn to the Islamic conception of God, of humanity, and of history. Then and only then can we turn our full attention to the role and the status of the Messenger and the Prophet in Islam, and thence reflect on the role of Jesus in the Christian and Islamic traditions. As we do so, beyond the fundamental differences that must, of course, also be underlined and analyzed, we will encounter numerous teachings held in common.

## The Meaning of Prophecy

The connection between the Creator and humanity in Islam is directly associated with the notion of Revelation, and of the "messages" sent to mankind. The first two human beings, Eve and Adam, have knowledge of the existence of God. He speaks to them, gives meaning to their lives and establishes both a framework for and imposes limitations upon their behavior. At the heart of creation provided for them, all is permitted with the exception of a tree that, in Islam, is described neither in the Qur'an nor the prophetic traditions (*ahadith*, sing. *hadith*): contrary to the Biblical version, it is not the tree of knowledge (of good and bad) and nothing is known of its essence. But this tree sets a limit, in cognizance of which the two first conscious beings will express dual recognition of the primacy of God, the present and creating Being, and of their own selves, as human beings respecting and adoring the Unique. Adam is a Prophet (*nabi*), the first, as God has spoken to him and caused him to bear the responsibility of faith. But just as clearly he is not a Messenger (*rasul*), the bearer of a Revelation that he must convey to his people or to humanity at large.[1]

From the very beginning then, God speaks to humans, addressing them as monotheists. Contrary to what has been propagated and repeated in history books shaped by certain sociological and philosophical presuppositions (where spiritual traditions and religions are concerned), humans did not come to monotheism by rising above, over time, their primitive polytheistic beliefs toward belief in a single God (as evidenced in Akhenaton among the Egyptians or Platonic intuition among the Greeks). Judaism, Christianity, and Islam agree that quite the opposite is true: human beings began with knowledge of God in His unicity and, over time, "fell"

---

1. The distinction is critical in the Muslim tradition: all Messengers are Prophets, but not all Prophets are Messengers. Noah, Abraham, Moses, Jesus, and Muhammad are Messenger-Prophets.

or "deviated" toward polytheism. Polytheism is thus historically secondary, the product of human forgetfulness and negligence. Such is human nature: human beings know, recognize, and respect, only to disregard, to neglect, and to forget. The prophetic cycles occur precisely to correct the imperfection that has accompanied humankind, in its fallible memory, from its origins. At irregular intervals God in His grace and His mercy sends to humanity, to certain peoples, or at specific historical moments, Messengers or Prophets whose essential role is to recall the presence of the Creator and the meaning of life.

Prophecy thus constitutes the unbroken link that the Eternal establishes with the temporal, the Creator with the awareness of the created, God with humanity. It has four essential functions:

1. To recall the presence of the Creator in His being, His eternity, His unicity and his non-representation (rejection of anthropomorphism).

2. To define the meaning of Creation and of life as established by the Creator: "We are from God and to Him is our return" (Q 2:156).

3. To confirm the rituals by which human beings respond to God's call and preserve its memory and the indispensible connection of their relationship as worshippers.

4. To correct that which human beings may have altered or perverted over time, as well as their interpretations of earlier Revelations.

From this perspective, Messengers or Prophets, irrespective of the time or the place where they are sent, will always have the four-fold role of recalling, defining, confirming, and correcting. It is through this prism that the Islamic tradition embraces all cycles of prophecy; all Messengers have exercised the same function, culminating in the last Messenger, Muhammad, the bearer of the final Revelation, which satisfies all four criteria while adding yet another: that the Qur'an brings these cycles to a close.

"Today have I perfected your religion for you, and have bestowed upon you the full measure of My blessings, and willed that self-surrender unto Me [Islam] shall be your religion" (Q 5:3). This verse of the Qur'an should be understood on two distinct levels. Muhammad's mission has ended and the last religion, Islam, is thereby established. But in a broader sense, it affirms the culmination of all Revelations, and Islam—in the generic sense of "entering into the Peace of God," as Abraham, Moses, and Jesus were *muslims* (at peace with the unique God, self-surrendering unto

Him)—is accepted as the religion of truth. This cannot be taken to mean that there will not be more than one religion, for God has willed diversity. But the final Revelation brings the historic recall to an end and declares that there will henceforth be neither Messenger nor Prophet (but only reformers down through the centuries).

Prophecy is thus a response to humanity's need to be summoned and to be reminded, so that men and women follow the Way laid down by the Creator. In terms of their reason, of their hearts, and their bodies, men and women stand in need of guidance so as not to go astray and thus act against themselves. Hence the attested need for Messengers and for a Message standing as an invitation to humility with regard to self, as well as to reverential love (*taqwa*) of God, and to faith and confidence (*iman*) in Him. In their search for truth, happiness, and peace, men and women are called upon to combine independence of mind with ontological dependence upon the Most High. Prophecy, in this light, reveals an idea of a God who accompanies humanity, which is capable of the worst, lest it forget, or of the best, as long as it remains committed to the revealed message, to the exemplary nature of the Messenger, and to the Way that the two together have taught it.

## God, Humanity, and History

Islam can be characterized as "demanding monotheism," to use Blachère's felicitous formula.[2] Indeed, the notion of *tawhid* (the unicity of God) is the axis around which all the teachings of Islam are articulated and understood. God is the Unique, the Most High, He who is "near" (Q 2:186), "closer to [to Man] than his jugular vein" (Q 50:16), "Creator of the heavens and the earth" (Q 35:1), "Lord of the worlds" (Q 43:46), of which He is the exclusive "owner" (Q 19:40), "Giver of life and death" (Q 17:58) for all living creatures. Humanity cannot partake of His essence, does not possess the faculties to conceive of His being, nor to conceptualize either what defines Him or what represents Him. "There is none like unto Him" (Q 112:4) that can be imagined, and nothing can be said of God but what God has revealed about Himself. There thus exists a fundamental difference, both in terms of nature and of essence, between the Divine (the Transcendent, and the immanence of the Transcendent in the mystical experience) and the human, irrespective of the form his or her spiritual experience may take.

2. Blachère, *Dans les pas de Mahomet*, 126.

God reveals Himself and offers Himself to the knowledge of humanity through His Revelations, which, down through history, have roused humans' awareness and made them attentive: "within the heavens and the earth are signs for the believers" (Q 45:3). These successive Revelations are the sources of light (*nur*) that form the bond between God, who is Light (one of God's names: *al-Nur*), and humanity, into whose heart the Creator has breathed His spirit (*ruh*). *Ruh*, the spirit, is not God, but can be likened to a spark that animates the human being and impels him or her, ontologically and naturally, to embark on a quest for Light, for God. This natural aspiration is known in the Muslim tradition as *al-fitra*: it provides a specific conception of humanity, whom everything differentiates from God but in whose heart God has placed a breath that invites him or her to the search for self and for the Transcendent, and that lends meaning to his or her life and to his or her presence on earth. The experience of faith thus becomes "light upon light" (*Nur 'ala nur*; Q 24:35), as the qur'anic Revelation so beautifully puts it, describing the meeting of the spark that seeks and the Divine that represents the very object of its search, the ultimate answer to the question of meaning. The meeting, the recognition that flows from it, up to and including fusion, quenches the thirst of whoever seeks meaning; their questions (the original spark) find their response (the Light). That state—the very experience of faith—is best expressed by a sense of peace (*salam*, one of God's names), of calm, and of security (one of the etymological meanings of faith, *iman*).

Humans are by their nature searching, in constant tension, at perpetual risk of imbalance and conflict with themselves, with their fellow human beings, and with the universe that surrounds them. They are needful beings and yet God, who has created them, has never left them to their own devices. God constantly makes Himself known through His Revelations and the signs of His presence in the Heavens, on the Earth, and within humanity. Calling and recalling, God summons humanity to inward peace, to peace with one another, and with all creation. To attain to this state the "children of Adam" must rise fully to their stature as human beings with humility, in recognition of the essential difference in nature between them and God. For it is Revelation, the word of God, that establishes—in making clear its meaning—the link (*religio*) between God, in His infinite and boundless Grace, and humanity, in its finitude, its needs, and its dependency. A qur'anic verse synthesizes the relation: "The Most Merciful/Taught the Qur'an/Created Man [and] taught him expression" (Q 55:1–4). Here, in the verse sequence itself, "Revelation" falls between "The Most Merciful" (one of God's names, which express His compassion toward humanity with which He communicates) and the creation of the human being.

In the Islamic tradition Revelation, whose ultimate expression, the Qur'an, is the word of God directly revealed "in a clear, understandable Arabic" (Q 16:103), creates a fundamental correlation between God and Humanity. It differentiates between beings Divine and human, and describes in detail the terms of their relationship. God is God, and nothing can be associated with Him. He has given human beings ways of seeking Him, of drawing near to Him, and even of knowing Him intimately but without ever pretending that they possess divine qualities. Humans are humans, with all their limitations.

The history of prophecy represents the unfolding, in time, of God's presence and of His recalling. Precisely those factors that summon human beings to preserve the bond, to remember God, and to draw near to Him in order not to go astray in their humanity, their imperfection, their instincts, and their negligence. The natural state of the human beings is tension, the search for meaning, need. But humans likewise possess the capacity to liberate themselves. Bearing within them a spark, surrounded by the signs of Creation and accompanied, throughout history, by a succession of Revelations—including those of the last three monotheisms—they may strive toward peace and to salvation on the three-fold condition that they assume their status with humility; that they conscientiously search for meaning, and that they deepen their knowledge of themselves and of the world.

## The Role and Status of the Messenger

We may now gain a fuller understanding of the role and the status of Messengers and Prophets in the Muslim tradition. Between the Divine, of which there is nothing comparable, and the human being who yearns for light and peace, the Prophet bears a message whose substance can be interpreted in two ways: through the content of the message itself, and through its translation, or more accurately, its full expression in the person of a living witness, through the behavior of the Messenger.

We have already discussed the content of the Revelations that recall to us the presence of the Unique, confirming the essence of faith and correcting what may have been altered or perverted. Messengers, it goes without saying, play an essential role in the understanding, the explication, and the initial exegesis of the Revelation they bear. They lend it meaning and depth and convey its spiritual, individual, and social implications. They enlighten, educate, and give direction.

On the personal level, Messengers are witnesses for the Message they bear. In this manner, according to the Muslim tradition, the vitality and the power of their function as witnesses derives from the fact that they are and remain human, with all the limitations that this implies. Of course, their lives may be marked by miracles, such as that of Abraham who survived the pyre, or Jesus and his birth, but they never depart from the bounds of their humanity: they live and die, their knowledge is limited, they have needs and instincts and may commit errors of judgment and action in everyday life (but not within the strict framework of their mission). They provide the prime example of the translation into human language of the spiritual message they bring, and it is precisely because they are only human beings like all those around them, as the Qur'an reminds us about the Prophet Muhammad, that their message takes on its full meaning: "indeed, in the Messenger of God, you have a good example" (Q 33:21). All Messengers possess this same status. So it is that the Muslim tradition recognizes Jesus while rejecting the idea that —in contrast to Christianity—he is the son of God and that he possesses a divine constitution that distinguishes him from other humans.

## Jesus as Prophet, and Islam

The Islamic position can be understood on the basis of the two fundamental principles that we have outlined. First, Islamic monotheism, which stands closer to Judaism, draws a fundamental distinction between Divine and human; the latter may never lay claim to the qualities of the former. Second, God "neither begets nor is begotten" (Q 112:3). He cannot have a son, and is beyond the temptation of anthropomorphism such as that connected with the idea of incarnation, a wholly foreign concept in Islam. The idea of the Trinity is presented in the Qur'an as a distortion of the original message of monotheism brought by Jesus and which Muhammad came to recall, to confirm, and to correct according to the teachings of the last of the revealed religions.

At the conclusion of Muhammad's prophetic mission, a situation arose that echoed the Christian tradition, but with a fundamental difference. Upon the Messenger's death, his Companion 'Umar was profoundly saddened and distraught. He could not bring himself to believe that the Prophet had indeed died, asserting that Muhammad was not dead, that he would be resuscitated, and that he—'Umar—would kill whoever dared declare him dead. At that moment another Companion, Abu Bakr, stepped forward: "And now, he who worships Muhammad, [know that] Muhammad is dead. But he who worships God, [know that] He is ever living and never dies."[3] He went on to recite verses that had already been revealed, which retroactively confirmed wisdom and lucid grasp of Islamic teachings: "Muhammad is not but a Messenger. Messengers have already passed away before him. If he dies or is killed will you turn back upon your heels? And whoever turns back upon his heels, he will by no means do harm to God in the least and God will reward the grateful" (Q 3:144). When he heard the verse, 'Umar realized that Abu Bakr was right, that Muhammad was but a man, and that he had departed this world.

According to the Islamic tradition, Jesus, the son of Mary, was conceived without a father. Throughout his life he performed miracles, and ranks high among the most eminent Messengers of the prophetic cycles. He brought the message of the Gospel, which is founded upon the unicity of God and points out the pathways to God's love. Jesus thus corrected the hypertrophy of the judicial and legalistic strictures that had, over time, shrunk the Jewish Torah to little more than a list of rulings and prohibitions. Jesus, too, recalled, defined, confirmed, and corrected. But, according to the Muslim tradition, he never claimed to be the "Son of God," nor God's incarnation, as any of the three hypostases would have it. Nor is he, for Muslims, the obligatory passage to salvation for human beings by way of redemption for the sins of the children of Adam after the fall. In fact, the notion of original sin does not exist in Islam: humanity is born innocent and it is through his unmediated relationship with God that he may find the path that leads to salvation and peace.[4]

## Beyond Divergences

Muslims share with Jews and Christians the idea of a single God, Creator of the universe and of humanity, to which He dispatched Messengers whose task it was to recall His presence, to transmit His teachings, and to guide human beings in their thoughts and their spirituality, as in their actions.

3. Reported by Sahih al-Bukhari, 62.19. See www.sunnah.com/bukhari/62/19.

4. For more on sin and the human condition, see chapter 7.

The three monotheisms that Islam describes as "religions of the Book" or "People of the Book" (*Ahl al-Kitab*) cannot otherwise be understood. Each tradition would develop its theological particularities, its rituals, its ethical system, and its praxis. But ultimately, the three monotheisms agree on the fundamental and historical importance of Prophecy and of its Messages. God speaks to human beings, making it possible for them to preserve the connection between the Transcendent and the temporal. Such is the function of Revelation; each of the three traditions was to be determined by a body of practices and ultimate goals designed to keep human faith alive.

We encounter fundamental differences between the traditions when we come to the role of Messengers and Prophets, and more specifically with regard to Jesus. Islam accords him a particular status by virtue of his birth, his miracles, and his return to earth as a sign of end times. But he is nonetheless a human Messenger who could not have been conceived by a virgin nor have performed miracles except by the will of the single God who breathed into him His spirit (but none of His divine attributes). He is—for Muslims—a human being sent to his fellow humans with a Message from God, like all the other Prophets before and after him.

The Christian tradition, in its various manifestations, is at odds with this understanding of the mission of Jesus. He is most certainly a Messenger but partakes, for the believer, of the very essence of God and of the path to salvation. Exactly the same meaning defines Christianity as a religion, in its doctrine and its institutions.

Divergences aside, however, it is indeed possible to point to a number of features shared by the Christian and Muslim traditions concerning Jesus and the meaning of his Prophecy. Once understood, it sets forth an idea of God that recalls to us His concern for humanity, His grace, His mercy, and His compassion. Like Messengers, these Messages are reminders, examples, gifts that show that God is, beyond all doubt, love. Never does He cease to lavish love upon His creatures, so that they turn toward Him in love. For at the core of Revelation lies the expression of God's benevolence toward humanity.

Such too is the role of Prophets. The Bible, which, in the New Testament, reports the life and times of Jesus, transmits to humanity the truth of faith in action. Jesus is a model, an educator, a teacher who illustrates to the faithful how belief can change a heart, transform the world, and lend courage to all those who keep that faith alive in their innermost being. Prophecy, in the three monotheistic traditions, fulfills the worthy function of edification.

Even though Christianity and Islam differ on a significant body of doctrine, common conclusions may be drawn from the life of Jesus in terms of devotion to God, to his mission as well as in his resistance to the powers of injustice, and of the courage of his convictions to the bitter end. The lives of Jesus and Muhammad echo each other. They abound in the same spiritual, social, and even political lessons: how to free oneself from all temporal powers in the name of service to the power of God alone. Jesus' rejection of political action is, in and of itself, an eminently political act, as indeed was his decision to make common cause with the poor and the downtrodden. From this perspective, the political action of the Messenger of Islam was far from the fascination of power, government, or domination but, on the contrary, to resist these things; to emancipate himself from them in the name of justice, of love, and of human dignity. The Prophet's life is itself the expression of spiritual and ethical counter-power.

Contrary to the often-repeated assertion that there exists a natural connection in the Islamic tradition between religion and political activity, between the Messenger and the political leader, Islam shares with Christianity an entirely different conception of political action, as evidenced by the Messenger. The sense of humility in the face of the ultimate power of God, the imperative of service to the poor and the orphan, the struggle against the corruption of power and money, are—each and every one—teachings found in the three monotheisms, and that must imperatively be put forward. The exemplary quality of the Messengers derives from their recognition of the power of God, and of the heart, their resistance to all dictatorial and financial power, and, in a more subtle sense, the power of instincts. Revelation is liberation, and the Prophet is the example of one who has freed himself, in history, from the chains that bound him.

## Conclusion

Close study of the role of prophecy in Islam is vital to grasp how its teachings have come to articulate the relation between God, the Message, the Messenger, and humankind. I have attempted to explain the meaning of prophecy both with regard to principles and from a historical perspective. Four functions—recall, define, confirm, and correct—have allowed me to explain why Revelations have followed one upon another, up until the final one, the Qur'an. We have understood that our reflection could not have been complete had we not examined the conceptions of God, of humanity, and of history in the Muslim tradition.

God, for Muslims, is present and makes Himself known to humankind, which is in a state of permanent tension and of necessity. Sacred history is that instant in time—the duration of a breath—that either brings creatures closer to or drives them further from their Creator. It is given form by the Revelations of which the Messengers and Prophets are living witnesses. They are merely humans, carried along by the power of faith and, on occasion, by those miracles that only God can bring about. They bear living witness to the teachings they have brought. Messengers point to the path of connection with God, with self, with humankind, with nature, and with all living creatures. They lend form and substance to devotion, to compassion, to service, and to courage in close company with God, in the service of humankind. Finally, they mark out the paths to salvation for the believer, of which Jesus is the necessary mediator for the Christian, while being one of the forms of its expression for the Muslim. If there is no salvation without Jesus for the Christian, there can be none for the Muslim if Jesus is not also its Messenger and witness.

# 5

# The Qur'an as God's Revelation in Christian-Muslim Relations

## Ayşe İçöz

*These are the verses of the clear book. Indeed, we have sent it down as an Arabic Qur'an that you might understand.* (Q 12:1–2)

*Indeed, it is We who sent down the Qur'an and indeed, We will be its guardian.* (Q 15:9)

This is how the core religious text of Islam describes itself. It is the direct, unchanged message of God that was revealed in clear Arabic language (Q 16:103; 26:95; 46:12). According to Muslim tradition, the sacred text was revealed to the Prophet Muhammad through the angel Gabriel in a process that took place in the span of twenty-three years.

From the earliest years on, several branches of religious sciences emerged around reading, understanding, and interpreting the Holy Scripture of Islam. The literature of *fadail al-Qur'an* touches upon various issues regarding the study of Islamic scripture such as the situation of Qur'an reciters in the Muslim society and Qur'an teaching. *'Ilm al-Qira'a* studies the various methods of Qur'an recitation. Memorizing the whole Qur'an is held as one of the most prestigious professions in the Muslim society. Following its revelation, the form of Arabic that is reflected in the Qur'an (*al-'Arabiyya al-Fusha*) was accepted as the purest and the most perfect form of the language. According to the traditional perception of medieval Muslim scholars, Arabic grammar was invented and improved in order to codify the language of the Qur'an to avoid any distortion or pollution.[1] Another linguistic concern of medieval Muslims was to understand and interpret the Qur'an accurately. Therefore, the intensive study of Arabic grammar and vocabulary was an indispensable element of qur'anic hermeneutics.[2]

When the science of systematic theology began to flourish around the mid-eighth century, discussions on the ontological status of the Qur'an as the "word of God" started within Muslim circles. The debate was attached to one of the most prominent discussions of Islamic theology: the divine attributes. Two major stances emerged regarding the interpretation of the principle of unity and the function and the status of the attributes of God. According to followers of the Mu'tazila school of thought, who were the advocators of reason in Islamic theology, in order to maintain pure *tawhid* and avoid the existence of any other eternal entities along with God, the hypostatic character of God's essential attributes such as power, life, will, and knowledge should be denied. These attributes are identical with God and inseparable from the divine essence. Thus, God knows, wills, or sees by his essence, or rather by the attributes of knowledge, will, and sight that are identical with His essence. The Mu'tazilites' main purpose was "purifying" (*tanzih*) God of all defects and of all plurality. They were accused of "robbing" (*ta'til*) God of His attributes by their opponents.[3]

These discussions on the attributes of God paved the way to the famous debate regarding the origins and the creation of the Qur'an as it is addressed as the "words of God" (*kalam Allah*) in the Qur'an (9:6; 48:15). In this case, the question was whether "the word" existed before God began creation. Following their strict interpretation of *tawhid*, Mu'tazilites argued that the answer was simply "no." Thus the Qur'an was created "in time" by God.[4]

The opponents of the Mu'tazilites on the ontological status of the Qur'an are usually associated with the followers of the renowned theologian Ahmad ibn Hanbal (780–855), though he is not the originator of this doctrine. He simply rejected asserting anything that is not directly and explicitly mentioned in the Qur'an. According to him, the Qur'an was neither creator (*khaliq*) nor created (*makhluq*). The followers of Ibn Hanbal held

---

1. For the birth of grammar, see the traditional account al-Anbari, *Nuzhat al-'adibba' fi tabaqat al-'udaba'*, 6.

2. Versteegh, *Landmarks*, 8–17.

3. Watt, *Formative Period*, 42.

4. Caspar, *Historical Introduction*, 178.

different views regarding what constitutes God's speech, but they agreed that God's words are eternal and thus uncreated, just like Him.[5]

As can be seen, the influence of Islamic scripture could be observed almost in every sphere of the social and intellectual life of the medieval Muslim society. In the Qur'an, Christians were classified under the title of *Ahl al-Kitab* (People of the Book) along with Jews and a few other religious groups who were considered as the possessors of earlier divine scriptures. The Qur'an assumes its audience to be familiar to the messages of the Torah and the Gospel. However, the original form of these divine revelations were corrupted (*tahrif*) and changed (Q 2:42, 59, 75–79; 3:71, 78; 4:46; 5:13, 41; 6:91; 7:162). The scripture of Islam denotes itself as the continuation of the original divine messages of these earlier revelations (Q 4:47; 5:46).

Given the qur'anic view of non-Muslim scripture, it might be expected that Arabic-speaking Christians would not only make use of the Qur'an but form their own views as well. After falling under Islamic rule from the seventh century onwards, Christians who lived in the Islamic caliphate found themselves in a society that was dominated and ruled by the principles of Islam that were mainly shaped by the teachings of the Qur'an and the tradition of the Prophet Muhammad. While they adjusted themselves to the new socio-political, intellectual setting under their protected status (stipulated in various forms under "dhimma" regulations), they also made an effort to protect and defend their faith against the criticism of Islam.

The most heated debates in Muslim-Christian polemics of this early period revolved around the doctrines of Trinity, Incarnation, and salvation.[6] The earliest known apology produced in Arabic appears in the mid-eighth century entitled *On the Triune Nature of God* (*Fi tathlith Allah al-wahid*) as an anonymous text that was preserved at St. Catherine's monastery in a single incomplete manuscript.[7] The text focuses on the subjects ranging from the doctrines of the Trinity, Incarnation, and salvation history and contains quotations from both the Bible and the Qur'an. In this earliest apology, the text reflects the author's awareness of the surrounding dominant culture that was conditioned and shaped by the teachings of the Qur'an in various ways. For example, the opening section of this apology is composed in rhymed prose (*saj'*) and contains several expressions borrowed from the Qur'an. In this way, it sounds very similar to Meccan suras. Samir Khalil

---

5. Tritton, "Speech of God." See also the discussion in chapter 8.

6. Waardenburg, *Muslim Perceptions*, 49.

7. See an excerpt in Tieszen, *Textual History*, 20–29.

Samir points to the author's spontaneous use of qur'anic terminology and connects it to the text's artistic features. He states that the author lived in a Muslim-dominated society that led him to be "impregnated" with the surrounding "qur'anic culture."[8] In his *Christian Exegesis of the Qur'an*, Scott Bridger argues that by using *saj'* and qur'anic expressions, the author of this apology aimed to have the same "rhetorical" and "emotional" impact on his listeners as they might with the Qur'an.[9] According to Sidney Griffith, the author's use of qur'anic material shows the "active currency" of the Qur'an within Christian circles and its "probative" impact in the writings of Arabophone Christian authors during the medieval period.[10]

Paul of Antioch's *Letter to a Muslim Friend* from the thirteenth century is a good example where the use of qur'anic verses in a polemical context can be observed throughout. The letter emerges following Paul's journey to Constantinople through the lands of the Byzantine Empire and to Rome. During his visits to these Christian territories, he had the opportunity to meet the significant personalities at various levels of society in these regions and ask their opinion about Islam and the Prophet Muhammad. He claims that the people whom he encountered had a copy of the Qur'an in hand and had examined it to see whether or not it was convincing.[11] Thus, the purpose of Paul's letter is to communicate their objections about Islam to a Muslim friend who inquires about the issue.

The letter contains numerous references to the Qur'an to justify Christian doctrines of the Incarnation and Trinity. According to the text, the Qur'an was sent only to the "pagan Arabs" and there is indeed an agreement between the Islamic scripture and the Bible on the idea that Christianity is the correct religion.[12] Throughout the letter, Paul provides a manipulative reinterpretation of the sacred text of Islam in order to impress his Muslim interlocutor. In the initial sections of his letter, Paul insists that Christians are the ones who follow the path of God and His revelation, citing numerous passages from the Qur'an on the miracles of Jesus, the purity of Mary, and the praiseworthy acts of the Christian community. The emphasis on

8. Samir, "Earliest Arab Apology," 109.

9. Bridger, *Christian Exegesis*, 100.

10. Griffith, *Church in the Shadow*, 56.

11 In the introduction to their edition and translation, Ebied and Thomas state that by the sound of their knowledge about Islam, it is very unlikely that these experts have the correct information and opinion about Islam. See Ebied and Thomas, eds., *Muslim-Christian Polemic*, 2.

12. Bulus al-Rahib al-Antaki, "Letter."

these passages is that the Qur'an confirms the truth of Christianity and the righteousness of Christians.[13] He is careful to interpret some of the qur'anic verses that contain more general expressions about the prophets and revelations according to his Christian agenda. This approach is very clear in his interpretation of Q 2:213 which states:

> Mankind was [of] one religion [before their deviation]; then Allah sent the prophets as bringers of good tidings and warners and sent down with them the Scripture in truth to judge between the people concerning that in which they differed. And none differed over the Scripture except those who were given it—after the clear proofs came to them—out of jealous animosity among themselves. And Allah guided those who believed to the truth concerning that over which they had differed, by His permission. And Allah guides whom He wills to a straight path.

According to Paul, "the prophets as bringers of good tidings" in this verse addresses Jesus and his disciples who spread his message to various lands rather than earlier Old Testament prophets who were sent for the Jews. This is mainly because the scripture (al-kitab) is mentioned in the singular form and it stands for the Gospel (Injil). In this case, Paul does not seem to be interested in clarifying the contradiction between the qur'anic expression of a single Gospel (Injil) and the Christian New Testament that consists of four Gospels. His discourse on Christian scripture sounds parallel to the qur'anic expression of the Gospel. According to the Qur'an, Jesus brought only one scripture (Injil) that was later corrupted. In the Qur'an, the word "Gospel" (Injil) always appears in singular form to address the original message of God that was revealed to Jesus (Q 3:3, 48, 65; 5:68).

The distinction between Jews and Christians appears more explicitly in the text when the author turns to recount various blameworthy acts of the People of Israel that are mentioned in the Old Testament.[14] He states that Christians never committed the acts that Jews did and they were also praised in the Qur'an: "You will surely find the most bitter towards the believers to be the Jews and polytheists and the most gracious to be those who call themselves Christian. That is because there are priests and monks among them and because they are not arrogant" (Q 5:82). It is very clear in this verse that Christians are separated from Jews and pagans and they are

13. Ibid., 54–69.
14. Ibid., 76–81.

mentioned next to "believers."[15] Clearly, Paul provides his own interpretation of these verses in favor of Christians regardless of traditional Muslim understanding and commentary.[16]

Medieval authors did not always use the Qur'an to support their apologetic agenda. They also made criticisms and challenged its divine origin. The treatise that is known as the "Risala" or the "Apology of al-Kindi" from the ninth century is a good example of this attitude.[17] It was written by a Christian from the well-known Christian Arab tribe of Kinda. The name of the author is not certain; he is known by the pseudonym of "Abd al-Masih ibn Ishaq al-Kindi." The apology is composed as a response to a letter that is written by a Muslim opponent, "Abdallah ibn Ismail al-Hashimi," to explain certain practices and beliefs of Muslims and invite al-Kindi to convert to Islam. In his answer, al-Kindi touches upon various issues regarding Islam and Christianity in order to defend his position and convince al-Hashimi to convert to his own religion.[18]

A certain portion of al-Kindi's response is devoted to addressing and criticizing various Muslim perceptions of the Qur'an. When compared to other Christian authors' engagement with the sacred text, al-Kindi's references to the Qur'an are more direct and explicit. Before turning to discuss different features of the Qur'an, he criticizes the miraculous status of the Qur'an for Muslims, comparing it with wonders that are performed by the earlier prophets such as cleaving the sea and raising the dead.[19]

The first issue that he examines regarding the Qur'an is the process of collection and compilation of the qur'anic manuscripts. Recounting some traditional narratives regarding the compilation of the Qur'an, al-Kindi argues that there are certain verses that are not included in the standardized Uthmanic codex.[20] By doing this, he first aims at refuting the Muslim assertion of a uniform and unchanged Qur'an.[21]

---

15. Ibid., 81–83.

16. For the use of qur'anic material in the original letter of Paul of Antioch see Wilde, *Approaches to the Qur'an*. For the full list of qur'anic verses used in the letter as it appears in the *Letter from the People of Cyprus*, a later expanded version of Paul's *Letter to a Muslim Friend*, see Ebied and Thomas, eds., *Muslim-Christian Polemic*, 508–11 (for an excerpt of the *Letter from the People of Cyprus*, see Tieszen, *Textual History*, 182–88).

17. See an excerpt in Tieszen, *Textual History*, 77–84.

18. Bottini, "Apology of al-Kindi."

19. Al-Kindi, *Risalat 'Abdallah*, 75–76.

20. Wild, "Canon."

21. Al-Kindi, *Risalat 'Abdallah*, 78–84.

The second issue to which al-Kindī devotes a lengthy passage is related to the linguistic features of the Qur'an. He writes:

> Now inform me about your master's saying "If all human beings and jinns strive to produce something similar to this Qur'an, they are not capable of bringing anything equal to it, even if some of them help the others" (Q 17:90). If you inquire whether there is any other language which is more eloquent (than Arabic), our answer will be "yes," Greek is the most eloquent language for Romans, Zend is for Persians, Syriac is for people of Edessa and Syria, and Hebrew of Jerusalem is for Jews. Indeed, every language seems more eloquent to its users than any other language. There are always eloquent words in each language for its users through which they communicate that sounds foreign to you, just like your Arabic sounds foreign to them.[22]

After evaluating the traditional Muslim perception of the miraculous status of the language of the Qur'an, he cites Q 12:2: "Certainly, we sent down the Qur'an in Arabic language thus you can understand it," and turns to recounting some of the foreign vocabulary in the sacred text that are of Persian and Abyssinian origin.[23] He states that the Arabic versions of these foreign words were available in the time of Muhammad as other Arab orators who lived before him, such as the poet Imru' al-Qais (d. 544), used the Arabic versions of these terms. Thus, recalling his earlier discussion on the process of collecting qur'anic manuscripts, al-Kindi reiterates that the blame should be placed on the other people who got involved in the process of compiling the sacred text for the employment of these foreign words.[24] In this case, he uses the assertion of the Qur'an to challenge its authenticity.

Another issue that al-Kindi mentions regarding the language of the Qur'an is the linguistic style of the text and the use of *saj'*. He states that this very style is not restricted to the qur'anic text only; there are many other poetic texts that employed the same rhetorical figures and the ornamental style. Moreover, Islamic scripture is not the most advanced version of this specific literary genre. According to al-Kindi, other poetic texts sound more eloquent and meaningful than the Muslim scripture while there is not a full integrity in the qur'anic suras.[25] As can be seen, al-Kindi focuses

22. Ibid., 85.
23. Ibid.
24. Ibid., 86.
25. Ibid., 86–87.

on disproving the Qur'an's validity in the eyes of Muslims, using qur'anic verses and traditional material.

The eighth century apologist and *mutakallim* Theodore Abu Qurra's employment of qur'anic verses to support his arguments during a series of discussions with some prominent Muslim figures of his time in the court of al-Ma'mun is one of the most creative examples of the employment of qur'anic material in a polemical context. A part of his encounter is related to theological discussions regarding the creation of the Qur'an. The debate revolves around the nature of Jesus. It starts when his adversary, Muhammad ibn Abdallah al-Hashimi, refers to Q 3:59 and 4:171. In the first verse Jesus is compared to Adam in terms of creation as they were both created from dust. In the second verse he is described as the "word" and "spirit" from God. Abu Qurra answers this statement with a series of questions regarding the origin of Jesus. He first asks whether the matter from which Adam was created is describable and measurable. After al-Hashimi's affirmative response, Abu Qurra inquires about the origins of Jesus, tricking him to refer to his second statement. Al-Hashimi states that he is created from the "word" and "spirit" of God. Abu Qurra continues asking whether the "word" and the "spirit" of God are depictable, describable, or measurable. Al-Hashimi responds negatively, stating that, since they are related to the essence of God, they are not even imaginable. At this point, Abu Qurra asks about the nature of the "word" of God: "Tell me about the word of God, is it creative or created?" This question silences al-Hashimi because if he answers "creative" he would lose the debate; however he was not prepared to state that the word of God is "created."[26]

Indeed, the very nature of the debate is closely linked to the contemporary *kalam* discussion concerning the createdness of the Qur'an mentioned above. The best way forward for al-Hashimi in this debate would be to affirm the created status of the "word of God." This simple statement would be appreciated by the caliph al-Ma'mun and release him from this unpleasant situation. But his reluctance to do so leads one to think that he was most likely to be on the side of those who claimed the uncreated status of the Qur'an. In this debate, Abu Qurra uses both qur'anic verses and the well-known theological discussion on the ontological status of the Qur'an in a very creative way. As Griffith remarks, the medieval Arabophone writers appear to be fully aware

---

26. Abu Qurra, *Mujadala*, 66–67.

of the impact and the influence of the Qur'an on Muslim communities and their perception of other religions and belief systems.[27]

Similar to their medieval counterparts, modern scholars show a nuanced approach regarding the utilization of the Qur'an in communication with Muslims. In the meeting of the Lausanne Committee for World Evangelization, the issue of using the Qur'an for the purpose of Christian dialogue with Muslims was addressed and five major tendencies were specified:

a.  The Qur'an should never be used in discussion with the Muslim, because using it implies that we accept it as inspired, and are putting it on the same level as the Bible.

b.  The Qur'an should be studied, but only to help us to know and appreciate what Muslims believe, and to enable us to learn Muslim terminology.

c.  The Qur'an should be used against itself, to demonstrate that it is self-contradictory. Such a polemical use of the Qur'an will show its weakness and create a hunger for something better.

d.  The Qur'an should be used as a starting point; e.g., the many verses that speak about Jesus and other biblical characters can be used to point to the biblical version of these same stories.

e.  The Qur'an can be used as a source of truth. Our recognition of all the truths that the Qur'an does contain makes the Muslim much less defensive and more open to read the New Testament.[28]

According to the statement, there are three major occasions where the positive use of qur'anic material is approved or encouraged. First, the Qur'an should be used to prove to Muslims its invalidity and self-contradiction, which sounds very similar to al-Kindi's medieval approach described above. Second, the commonalities between the Bible and the Qur'an should be highlighted in order to direct the Muslim audience's attention to the Bible. Third, acknowledging certain aspects of the Qur'an can help to gain Muslim counterparts' sympathy and encourage them to read the Bible. These major attitudes can be observed in various ways in the modern writings of Christian authors. Currently, Christian use of the Qur'an covers a wide span of genres from apologetic and polemical works to Qur'an commentaries. The authors vary in their approach and style in

27. Griffith, *Church in the Shadow*, 56.

28. Lausanne Movement, "Christian Witness to Muslims."

their writings according to their target audiences and the cultural backgrounds from which they come.

Among the modern examples of the use of Qur'an in Christian writings, Italian cleric Giulios Basetti-Sani is worth mentioning here as an example. According to him, the Qur'an should be examined considering its historical, cultural, and linguistic context.[29] The message of the Qur'an is not necessarily incorrect, but it should be understood as a preliminary text that was revealed to pagans in order to prepare them for the message of Jesus.[30] Therefore, the scripture of Islam could be only comprehended and appreciated through a "Christian key."[31] Thus, the teachings of the Qur'an do not really contradict the basic principles and doctrines of Christianity such as the Trinity. Conversely, the Qur'an affirms them.

In order to support this view, Basetti-Sani quotes several verses from the Qur'an. For example, Q 4:171–172, where the Christian belief in *tathlith* (i.e., Trinity) is rejected, becomes for Basetti-Sani affirmations of the Trinity:

> O People of the Scripture, do not commit excess in your religion or say about Allah except the truth. The Messiah, Jesus, the son of Mary, was but a messenger of Allah and His word which He directed to Mary and a soul [created at a command] from Him. So believe in Allah and His messengers. And do not say, "Three;" desist—it is better for you. Indeed, Allah is but one God. Exalted is He above having a son. To Him belongs whatever is in the heavens and whatever is on the earth. And sufficient is Allah as Disposer of affairs. Never would the Messiah disdain to be a servant of Allah, nor would the angels near [to Him]. And whoever disdains His worship and is arrogant—He will gather them to Himself all together.

Basetti-Sani is aware that Muslim scholars interpret these verses as disapproving of the Trinity. According to his alternative interpretation, the direct interlocutors of the verse that are addressed as "People of the Scripture" at the beginning are "Jews" who constantly criticized the Trinity by making up stories and yelling "three, three" to ridicule the Christian community whenever they met them. Also, they did not accept the messianic status of Jesus. Q 4:171 addresses these rejections and blames Jews who "commit excess" in their religion. In the second sentence of Q 4:171—"The

---

29. Basetti Sani, *Il Corano Nella Luce*, 33

30. Ibid., 224.

31. Ibid., 199.

Messiah, Jesus, the son of Mary, was but (*innama*) a messenger of Allah . . ."—the Arabic word "*innama*," which is interpreted as "but, no more than [a messenger]" by Muslim *mufassirun*, is translated as "certainly" by Basetti-Sani. Consequently, according to his translation, the meaning of the verse turns to "Christ Jesus the son of Mary was *certainly* an apostle of Allah, and His Word, which he bestowed on Him, and a spirit proceeding from Him." According to him, the true meaning of this verse affirms the Trinity, as Christ is described as an apostle of God, His word and spirit. He interprets the following expression "say not three" in the verse as a warning to Jews to prevent them from ridiculing the Christian Trinity.[32]

The commentary by Carol Ghattas and her Egyptian husband Paul Ghattas entitled *A Christian Guide to the Qur'an* is worth mentioning here since the authors had very close contact with Muslims as missionaries in the Middle East and North Africa. In the introduction of their commentary, a brief background regarding the life of the Prophet Muhammad and the revelation of the Qur'an is given according to the traditional Muslim perception and narratives.[33] Their interpretation deals with each sura of the Qur'an separately under relevant titles. At the end of the book, some information is provided in three appendices entitled "Brief Outline of Important Dates in Islam," "Biblical Names Found in the Qur'an," and "Biblical References by Topic." The purpose of the commentary is to provide some guidance to Christians regarding the Qur'an for their missionary efforts. Before moving to the main body of the commentary, the readers are warned to maintain close contact with the Bible in order to avoid possible attacks of the "Evil One."[34]

Each section contains a brief outline of the relevant sura, and then starts examining certain verses. The commentary sections explain how a selected verse could be used to draw the Muslim interlocutor's attention to the Bible. For example, in the first chapter, which deals with Q 1, the sixth verse in which the "straight path" is mentioned, Christian readers are advised to recite John 14:6 where the "Christian" straight path is explained: "I am the way, the truth and the life."[35]

The authors also object to the perception of the Qur'an as a unique miraculous book. They encourage Christian readers to compare and contrast

32. Ibid., 200–207.

33 Though they use some modern scholarly sources for reference in this section.

34. Ghattas, *Christian Guide*, 14.

35. Ibid., 18.

the linguistic features of the Qur'an and pre-Islamic poetry in order to challenge Q 2:23 where unbelievers are challenged to bring a similar sura.[36] In this way, each chapter examines a sura focusing on certain verses that can be relevant to use for missionary purposes.

Scott Bridger's *Christian Exegesis of the Qur'an* can be mentioned as a final example here. Bridger bases his approach on the use of Greek philosophy in Acts 17. He states that Paul's knowledge and familiarity with Athenians' worldview enabled him to communicate a "biblical" message to Athenian pagans.[37] Similarly, Christians who target Muslim audiences can use qur'anic expressions and ideas to convey the Bible's message to Muslims. In his book, Bridger examines the use of qur'anic material in both medieval and contemporary Christian Arabic writings that emerged in Muslim-dominated regions. The aim is to enter the Qur'an's "hermeneutical circle," trying to draw Muslims into the Bible's "hermeneutical horizon." According to Bridger, the Qur'an should be detached from the interpretations of traditional Muslim *mufassirun*, and its expressions should be reinterpreted according to biblical perspectives for fruitful results in missiological efforts.[38] For this purpose, Bridger points to the scholarly works of Wansbrough[39] and Reynolds[40] that highlight the biblical background of the Qur'an.[41] Bridger's approach contains a comprehensive scholarly analysis of the use of the Qur'an in Christian apologetics and it provides a sophisticated missiological strategy.

Just like medieval authors, modern writers are aware of the impact of the Qur'an on Muslim communities. Thus, many of the Christian writers who target Muslim audiences refer to the Qur'an and see the Islamic scripture as a "bridge" to reach Muslims. Fouad Accad,[42] Kenneth Cragg,[43] and Corrie Block[44] are just few such writers to mention here. Their approaches are similar to the medieval writers; some of them use the qur'anic verses to support their arguments, some of them challenge its divine origins, and

---

36. Ibid., 21.

37. Bridger, *Christian Exegesis*, 44–47.

38. Ibid., 158.

39. Wansbrough, *Qur'anic Studies*.

40. Reynolds, *Qur'an and Its Biblical Subtext*.

41. Bridger, *Christian Exegesis*, 152–54.

42. Accad, *Building Bridges*.

43. Cragg, *Mind of the Qur'an*.

44. Block, *Qur'an in Christian-Muslim Dialogue*.

some engage with the Qur'an in the light of contemporary scholarly debates surrounding it. When compared to earlier apologetics, modern authors seem to adjust themselves to the social and intellectual dynamics of Muslim societies and produce a wide range of texts. Their ethnic and geographical background have an impact on their use of Qur'an and the way they engage with Muslim communities. Most of the medieval and contemporary authors provide their own interpretation of the verses neglecting the conformity of their interpretations to traditional Muslim exegesis. This raises the question of how far these interpretations would be acceptable and convincing within Muslim circles.

## 6

# Jesus as God's Revelation in Christian-Muslim Relations

## JOHN AZUMAH

JUDAISM, CHRISTIANITY, AND ISLAM have collectively been referred to in various ways including, Abrahamic religions, monotheistic religions, revealed religions, or prophetic religions. Some of the things these three religious traditions share in common are belief in one God (monotheism) and revelation (how the one God communicates with humankind). Having said that, the most profound differences between the three religions always lay just below the surface in the areas of apparent intersections. This is particularly so with the beliefs in the oneness of God and revelation. The understanding of who God is as well as the mode, content, and purpose of revelation is at the heart of some of the deepest differences between the three traditions. In this chapter, I am going to explore the topic of revelation from a Christian perspective, first with a brief general statement on a traditional Christian understanding of the doctrine of revelation. I will then go on to explore the New Testament, especially the Gospels' witness to Jesus as God's revelation. The distinguishing features of how God reveals Godself, God's will, and God's divine providence to humankind in Jesus for Christians will be highlighted. The key intersections with Islamic teaching will be noted and possible areas of dialogue lifted up.

## Revelation in Christianity

The Bible talks about revelation through various means. There are references in the Old Testament to revelation from nature (Ps 18:13, 19:1, 29:3), visions (Exod 33:22, Num 24:4, Isa 6), and dreams (Gen 28:11–15, 1 Sam 28:6). However, in the Old Testament revelation is mainly understood as direct hearing of God's Word (cf. Isa 5:9; Jer 23:18, 22) and indirectly as the perception of God's activity in the history of individuals (Ps 3; 118:13–29), and of the nation (Exod 15:1, Ps 98:2, Jer 33:16). Revelation is also regarded eschatologically in terms of the complete manifestation of God and the culmination of his purposes on "the day of the Lord" (Hos 2:19–23, Jer 31:34).

In the New Testament, revelation occasionally refers to the miraculous reception of supernatural knowledge (Matt 11:27; 16:17; Gal 2:2; 1 Pet 1:12). The dominant use of the concept refers to that future event in which God finally discloses himself (1 Cor 13:12; 1 John 3:2), or God's eschatological agent, the Messiah (Luke 17:30; 1 Cor 1:7; Rev 1:7), in judgment and salvation (Rom 8:18–38; 1 Cor 3:13; 1 Pet 1:5). It is an event which the early community of faith perceived to have been affected already in the life, work, death, and resurrection of Jesus of Nazareth (John 3:17ff., 9:39; Rom 1:17; Heb 9:26; 1 Pet 1:20).

Revelation in Christian thought therefore generally refers to the disclosure of what was previously unknown or only partially perceived. A key feature of revelation in Christian theology is that God is normally regarded as the agent of such disclosure and human beings the subjects who receive the revelation. "If God is to be known by limited, sinful humanity, God must 'reveal' or communicate the divine self in ways that humans can understand. This 'uncovering' of the God who is hidden, beyond human perception or understanding, is a disclosure of the divine."[1] The unveiling by God of what was previously concealed (in the past, present, or future) in revelation has traditionally been understood in terms of verbal or quasi-verbal communication by God to human recipients (prophets) who then pass on what they have received. The common biblical refrain is "Thus says the Lord . . ." in which revelation takes a propositional form, scripture literally taken to be the revealed word of God. This view has widely given way to the view that divine revelation takes place through specific events in history, and scripture, under the inspiration of the Holy Spirit, is a human record of such events.

---

1. McKim and Chung, "Revelation and Scripture."

In Christian theology, the Bible is the means or vehicle of divine communication with humanity. The idea of inspiration of scripture stems from such biblical passages as "All Scripture is God-breathed and is useful for teaching, rebuking, correcting, and training in righteousness" (2 Tim 3:16). The Greek word translated "God-breathed" (*theopneustos*) suggests the activity of the Holy Spirit (*pneuma*). Elsewhere in the New Testament, the Holy Spirit is said to have "moved" or carried along those who delivered prophecies (2 Pet 1:20–21). This divine and human engagement, partnership, or dialogue is a recurring dialectic in Christian theology, especially as it relates to our topic under consideration here. With this understanding of Scripture, the Bible is not considered in traditional Christian thought as the literal revealed word of God, but a divinely inspired human record of God's engagement with the world. Divine inspiration, rather than dictation of Scripture, allows for the divine and human origins of the Bible.[2]

Biblical inspiration is about the Holy Spirit, using or working through the authors of the different parts of the Bible without setting aside their personalities and faculties or divorcing them from their socio-political and cultural contexts. The Bible is therefore not the literal, eternal, revealed Word of God in traditional Christian thought as the Qur'an is understood in Islam. Rather, for Christians the Bible is an account of God's interaction with and through the people of Israel, of God's personal and direct involvement in and through the person, life, death, and resurrection of Jesus Christ, and of God continuing to work through the Holy Spirit in the lives and deeds of the early Christians. Together the *divine agency* in communication, disclosing and the *human agency* in receiving, preserving, and witnessing to what has been communicated are key to understanding the concept of scripture and revelation in Christianity.

Historically, revelation has been categorized in Christian thought into "general revelation" and "special revelation." Sometimes also referred to as "natural revelation," general revelation is, on the one hand, God's self-disclosure and communication in the universe and created order (Ps 19:1–6; Rom 1: 19–20). Special revelation, on the other hand, is God's self-disclosure and communication in specific times and places, "particularly in the events of Israel's history and, for Christians, in the person of Jesus Christ."[3] Shirley Guthrie offers the following classical clarification on general and special revelation:

2. Azumah, "Divine and Human Origins."
3. McKim and Chung, "Revelation and Scripture," 758.

General revelation refers to the self-disclosure of God that all people can perceive by contemplating evidences of God's presence in the world of nature, history, and human life in general. The knowledge of God derived from this revelation is sometimes called the natural knowledge of God. The movement of theological reflection here is from us to God; we seek God. Special revelation, on the other hand, refers to the unique self-revelation of God through God's word and action (1) in the history of Israel and above all in Jesus Christ, (2) through the Bible, which tells us of the God who came to us in this way, and (3) through the Christian church, which preserves and interprets the biblical witness. The knowledge of God derived from this source is called the revealed knowledge of God. The movement of theological reflection here is from God to us; God seeks and finds us.[4]

God is both the source and agent in general and special revelation. General and special revelation contain information and knowledge on aspects of God's character, will, and purposes, and about humanity in its relationship with God. The created order, which forms part of general revelation, was itself spoken into existence through the creative power of God's Word. The common refrain in the creation account in Genesis 1 is "And God said, 'Let there be . . . ,'" "And there was . . . ." The Psalmist testifies to the creative power of God's Word in the following words: "By the word of the Lord were the heavens made, and all the host of them by the breath of his mouth" (Ps 33:6). The same Word of God proclaimed through the mouths of the prophets shaped the course of the history of biblical Israel.

The Christian claim is that the eternal Word of God through which the universe was called into being, out of nothing (*ex nihilo*), and spoken by the prophets at a point in history took up residence in human form among humanity as Emmanuel, God with us. This is the process the writer of the book of Hebrews describes:

> In the past God spoke to our ancestors through the prophets at many times and in various ways, but in these last days he has spoken to us by his Son, whom he appointed heir of all things, and through whom also he made the universe. The Son is the radiance of God's glory and the exact representation of his being, sustaining all things by his powerful word. After he had provided purification for sins, he sat at the right hand of the Majesty in heaven. (Heb 1:1–3)

4. Guthrie, *Christian Doctrine*, 40.

The revelatory process moved from universality in general revelation to particularity in God's dealings with biblical Israel, and then to finality in Jesus Christ as Messiah, Son of Man, Son of God, and God with us. It is this process we now proceed to examine through the lens of the canonical Gospel accounts written by eyewitnesses and early disciples of Jesus: Matthew, Mark, Luke, and John.

## Portraits of Jesus in the Gospels

The word "gospel," from the Greek word *euangelion,* means "good news," used in the Greco-Roman world to denote the public, oral declaration of "good news," especially of victory in a battle.[5] The term was adopted in early Christianity to mean "good news" of or about Jesus Christ. In the Gospel accounts, "Jesus proclaims a message from God concerning the dawning messianic age, but by his words and deeds Jesus is the good news. He speaks God's word to the people; he is the message he proclaims."[6] The Gospel of Mark, considered to be the earliest of the four accounts, begins as follows: "The beginning of the good news about Jesus the Messiah" (Mark 1:1). In other words, Jesus himself—his birth, mission, death, and resurrection—is the "good news" that the writers of the Gospels sought to document and to which they meant to testify.

Accounts of Jesus in Matthew, Mark, and Luke are known as the Synoptic Gospels, "synoptic" meaning "shared or similar perspectives." These three accounts have a lot in common so New Testament scholarship came to regard them as drawing from a common source with specific details and emphases on the life of Jesus for their respective audiences. That Jesus lived, ministered (mainly teaching and healing), and was crucified in Palestine during or around the reign of the Roman governor Pontius Pilate are historical facts attested to in the synoptic accounts and in early Jewish and Roman sources. In other words, Jesus was indeed a man who walked upon the face of the earth and not a mythical figure. The dogmatic significance of events around Jesus and his activities are what the synoptic writers tried to elucidate. The portraits of Jesus in these accounts are generally explained as having to do with the target audience of each of the writers rather than disagreements or contradictions in the narratives.

5. Carroll, *Jesus and the Gospels,* 28.
6. Shenk, "Gospel," 357.

The Gospel account written by John bears features that make it distinct from the Synoptic accounts, but lest we think that John is too far removed from the Synoptic authors, it is intriguing to note that both in his purpose statement and throughout his Gospel, with a fair degree of frequency, the titles Christ or Messiah and Son of God (or simply Son) appear exactly as they do in Mark's headline (Mark 1:1). John goes on to clarify that the function of his account is that, "you may believe that Jesus is the Messiah, the Son of God, and that by believing you may have life in his name" (20:31). Thus, in John, as in the Synoptic Gospels, Jesus is both the Christ (the Messiah, the Anointed deliverer of Israel) and the Son of God (the one with a unique and uniquely intimate relationship, or sonship, with his heavenly Father).

A distinctive title for Jesus is in John 1:29 where John the Baptist declares Jesus as "the Lamb of God who takes away the sins of the world." This has the Old Testament background in terms of the Passover lamb—a sacrificial offering to denote forgiveness of sins and take the place of humans who deserve to die for their sins. But also, it is alluding to the sheep led to the slaughter in the context of the Suffering Servant texts and predictions in Isaiah, particularly Isaiah 53. The theme of the Suffering Servant found in the Synoptics is therefore also at the heart of John's Gospel. John's Gospel therefore has some of the most human portrayals of Jesus. Jesus experiences fatigue (4:6) and anguish of his impending death (12:27); he weeps at his friend Lazarus' death (11:33) and changes his mind (7:1-10). He is Jesus of Nazareth, the son of Joseph, "the one Moses wrote about in the Law and about whom the prophets also wrote" (1:44).

At the same time, Jesus has a very special relationship with God as Father. Jesus frequently refers to God as his Father and talks about "my Father, whom you claim as your God" (John 8:54). In John 3:16, he is the "only Son of God." Jesus goes a step further to declare "I and the Father are one" (John 10:30) and "he who has seen me has seen the Father" (John 14:9). Jesus even goes to the extreme to announce that "before Abraham was, I am" (John 8:58), to the chagrin of his audience. The most distinctive of John's Gospel, however, is he alone calls Jesus the Word (the *Logos*). The Greek term *logos* had a remarkably broad usage and application. In Jewish circles, it was the term often used to represent God's spoken word, through which creation itself was brought into being. Thus, unlike Matthew who traces Jesus back to Abraham, and Luke to Adam, John writes:

In the beginning was the Word, and the Word was with God, and the Word was God. Through him all things were made; without him nothing was made that has been made. In him was life, and that life was the light of all mankind . . . the Word became flesh and made his dwelling among us. We have seen his glory, the glory of the one and only Son, who came from the Father, full of grace and truth. (1:1–14)

"In the beginning" is a deliberate allusion to Genesis 1:1, while "the Word became flesh and made his dwelling among us" seems to be an echo of Matthew's Emmanuel, "God with us." Jesus is therefore the Son of Joseph, Son of God, and God himself in the Gospel of John.[7] It is in John's Gospel that we find the clearest enunciation of the Christian doctrine of incarnation, which is not about elevating a man, Jesus, into God. "The direction, so to speak, is 'upward,' from mundane to celestial. The whole meaning of the Christian recognition of Christ is totally contrasted. It has to do with the condescension of God in love to mankind."[8] One of the dominant emphases, therefore, for John's Gospel is Jesus as Revealer of God the Father. Jesus is God's revelation and therefore "Jesus is understood not only as bringing a teaching—as indeed he did—but as himself personifying what God reveals. He is not only an 'emissary' but the personality in and through whom God is known."[9]

When it comes to traditional Christian teaching on revelation, the divine and human factors are fully acknowledged as crucial and central. From the portraits of Jesus in the four Gospel accounts, we see that the humanity of Jesus is therefore fully attested. At the same time, we see the confession of Jesus as more than a rabbi and a prophet. From very early on, his disciples confessed him as the Messiah, the Son of God, and finally as God. The disciples "came to their conviction about 'God in Christ' because they acknowledged the 'Christ in Jesus' and in 'Jesus crucified.'"[10] The Christological controversies of the first five centuries of Christian history on some occasions were to affirm the true humanity of Jesus. Others were to affirm his full divinity. Hence, it was eventually resolved that Jesus is fully man *and* fully God or truly man *and* truly God. To confess Jesus as only divine is heretical just as it is to confess him as only human.

7. Kärkäinen, *Christology*, 41.

8. Cragg, *Jesus and the Muslim*, 203.

9. Ibid., 192.

10. Ibid., 193.

## Differences and Intersections with Islam

From the foregoing, it becomes clear that the difference between the Islamic and Christian understandings of revelation is the *nature* and *purpose* of the revelation. It should be pointed out that most traditional Islamic and Christian teachings agree on the eternal or uncreated nature of God's Word. The difference is that while much Islamic teaching stops at the point of affirming the uncreatedness of God's Word in the Qur'an with the words *bila kayfa* ("without asking how"), Christian teaching goes on to affirm that the eternal Word of God in Jesus cannot be other than God. In other words, while the concretizing of God's Word takes the form of *Text* and a *Book* in Islam, in Christianity it takes the form of *Flesh* and a *Person* in Jesus. Daniel Madigan explains the Christian witness contained in the Prologue to John's Gospel:

> "The Word was made flesh and pitched his tent among us;" that is to say, God's Word was spoken to us in an *embodied* language, or even, we might say, in body language. It is essential to understanding the Christian notion of the incarnation—the term derives from this very verse of John—to think of "flesh" as a language rather than as simply the body of a speaker. And when we speak of "flesh" in this case, Christians do not mean only a body, but rather a human person, the person of Jesus of Nazareth. The Word is expressed not simply through the words of the person Jesus but through his being and action. His entire life—the living, the dying, and the rising—is the message; he is for Christians not simply the messenger.[11]

For Christians, Jesus is the Word of God, the revelation of God, the gospel, the embodied language in which God communicated and engaged with humanity. Since God is eternal, his Word must be eternal, and if God's Word is eternal, the Word cannot be other than God. Otherwise, we end up with two eternal entities that will be irreconcilable with monotheism.

Responding to the notion of "God willing and wanting to reveal himself to man," Isma'il al-Faruqi spelled out the nature of revelation in Islam: "God does not reveal Himself. He does not reveal Himself to anyone in any way. God reveals only His will." Al-Faruqi goes on to explain further: "Christians talk about the revelation of God Himself—by God of God—but that is the great difference between Christianity and Islam. God is transcendent, and once you talk about self-revelation you have hierophancy and

---

11. Madigan, "Particularity, Universality," 18.

immanence, and then the transcendence of God is compromised. You may not have complete transcendence and self-revelation at the same time."[12]

In other words, al-Faruqi is claiming that God reveals only his will not his nature or himself as Christians claim. But as Kenneth Cragg cautions, "the nature/will distinction must not be pressed too far, since neither can be within our knowing without the other."[13] Madigan observes rightly that what Christians are doing in confessing Jesus as the Word of God, "is not different from what Muslims are doing. We are both recognizing the presence and expression of the eternal, universal, divine Word in something that, to someone who does not believe, is merely human—in the case of Christians, in a first-century carpenter from Nazareth; in the case of Muslims, in a seventh-century Arabic text."[14]

Even if we accept the received Muslim commentaries that the title of *Kalimatulla* ("Word of God") used in the Qur'an for Jesus refers to his conception by the power of the creative Word of God, thereby underscoring his createdness, the term is used only of Jesus in the Qur'an and no other created being. Indeed, the Qur'an simply states that "Jesus . . . was only a Messenger of God, and His Word that He committed to Mary, and a Spirit from Him" (Q 4:171). As rightly observed by Merad Ali, "The text does not say: 'Christ is only the apostle of God, born of His Kalima' but clearly: 'the apostle of God and His Kalima.' In the second verse, it is not stated: 'God gives thee glad tidings of a child produced by His Kalima,' but rather 'the good tidings of a Kalima from Him.'"[15]

In other words, the Qur'an, without the received commentaries, suggest that Jesus has a special relationship with the Word of God beyond giving voice to it as a messenger. Fully aware of the repeated denials in the Qur'an that Jesus is neither Son of God nor God, Merad notes that,

> In the Qur'an, the term *bashar* is distinctly applied to earthly humanity, in opposition to the world of spirits. Thus, for instance, the Prophet Muhammad declares several times, as far as he is concerned, he is only a man like other men, an ordinary mortal (Q 17:93; 18:110; 41:6). In this respect, it is remarkable that at no time

12. Al-Faruqi, "On the Nature," 47–48.

13. Cragg, *Jesus and the Muslim*, 192.

14. Madigan, "Particularity, Universality," 19.

15. Ali, "Christ selon le Coran," 85 ("*Or, le texte ne dit pas: 'le Christ est seulement l'Apôtre de Dieu, né de Sa Kalima;' il dit bien: 'l'Apôtre de Dieu et Sa Kalima.' Dans le second verset, il n'est pas dit: 'Dieu t'announce la bonne nouvelle d'un enfant produit par Sa Kalima,' mais plutôt: 'la bonne nouvelle d'une kalmia de Lui.'"*).

is the term *bashar* applied to Christ. And yet, it seems obvious that this would have been the best argument to weaken the notion of Christ's divinity and to put him forward under the guise of an ordinary mortal.[16]

In other words, the Qur'an raises more questions when it comes to Jesus and does not merely issue definitive declarations. These questions offer room for curiosity and dialogue between Muslims and Christians on the nature of Jesus and revelation.

Another important difference between the two traditions has to do with the *purpose* of revelation. The Qur'an refers to itself and earlier scriptures as "guide" (*huda*). "Ramadan is the [month] in which was sent down the Qur'an, as a guide to mankind, also clear [Signs] for guidance and judgment [Between right and wrong]" (Q 2:185; cf. 2:2–5). For many Muslims, the primary purpose of the Qur'an, therefore, is to provide guidance to humankind in the form of information and knowledge through education. Islamic mission (*da'wa*), to use the words of al-Faruqi, "is therefore an invitation to think and argue. It cannot be met with indifference except by the cynic, nor with rejection except by the fool or the malevolent."[17] With guidance as the purpose of revelation, it makes sense that the Word of God in Islam is a *text*, a *book*.

Asked why God would choose to use "body language" in Christianity, which can be vague and easily misunderstood instead of speech, Madigan explains that it depends on the message or purpose of the revelation God is intending to convey.

> If the message consists of direction and instruction, then the more straightforward the language is the better. If, however, the message is of love, forgiveness, and reconciliation, then as human beings we recognize that our gestures, our actions, our vulnerability—that is to say, our body language—speaks much more clearly than the finest of words . . . . The Word of God that Christians perceive to be revealed in Jesus is not a series of directives that need to be stated

---

16. Ibid., 87–88 (*"En effet, dans le Coran, le terme* bachar *est bien distinctif de l'humanité terrestre, par opposition au monde des esprits. C'est ainsi que, pour sa part, le prophète Muhammad proteste maintes fois qu'il est seulement un homme comme les autres, un simple mortel [Coran XVII, 93; XVIII, 110; XLI, 6]. Il est remarquable, à cet égard, qu'à aucun moment le terme* bachar *n'est appliqué au Christ. Il semble évident, pourtant, que c'eût été le meilleur argument pour infirmer la conception de la divinité du Christ, et pour présenter celui-ci sous les traits d'un simple mortel"*).

17. Al-Faruqi, "On the Nature," 34.

in clear unambiguous terms. It is the revelation of God's gracious, forgiving love. Talk is cheap, we rightly say, especially if it is talk about love. To embody love, on the other hand, costs everything.[18]

What Christians call the sacrificial or costly love, forgiveness, and reconciliation constitute the core message of the Christian Gospel, that is, Jesus. The disciples of Jesus believed him to have embodied the sacrificial love of God in his life, ministry, death, and resurrection. Madigan is therefore right that, in the Christian tradition, the revelation of God in Jesus is not a set of directives, but the outpouring of God's love and undeserved favor on an erring humanity. Of course, this is not to imply that love is not part of revelation in Islam or that guidance is unimportant to Christian witness. These points are made to underscore the idea that it may be in our perceived deepest differences that our commonalities are found, and that the same differences hold more potential for constructive dialogue than we may imagine.

18. Madigan, "Particularity, Universality," 20.

*7*

# Sin and Redemption in Christianity and Islam

## COSMAS EBO SARBAH

BOTH CHRISTIANS AND MUSLIMS are beset with a common human condition that is generally characterized by evil, suffering, and sin. Humanity seems to be menaced or oppressed by death, sin, law, and demonic forces, which appear in different shades and colors. There is enough evidence of bondage to evil forces on a national and international scale: uncontrollable greed, exploitation, institutional injustice, the arms race, revenge attacks, and violence of all kinds. Human beings, contaminated by sin and guilt, find themselves in an impure state. Hard-heartedness and cold indifference towards the sufferings of others, rampant fear, failure to forgive, and institutionalized hatred all point to something amiss within the human condition.[1]

In much of Christian thought, sin and the damaged human condition, often attributed to the first human being, Adam, is expressed in the doctrine of original sin.[2] The doctrine of original sin points to a basic solidarity in sin. It recalls the fact that all human beings are born into a bad environment. Besides involving a sin situation, original sin also entails some "alienation" from the Creator. Because of this present state of the human race, people are born affected by universal sin and deprived of the benefits of grace. This bad situation and state of deprivation in which

1. O'Collins, *Interpreting Jesus*, 136. See also Ricoeur, *Symbolism of Evil*, 25–46.

2. The Eastern Christian view differs from much of Protestant and Roman Catholic thought in its conception of original sin or inherited guilt and subsequent effects on humanity. For a summary, see Ware, *Orthodox Church*, 216–18.

individuals find themselves obviously could not be due to their personal bad choices. However, as a result of their personal sins, human beings ratify what they have inherited.[3] Redemption by Christ, then, is the Christian response to original sin and the inherited sin condition.

The Christian doctrine of original sin and redemption offers a more fundamental religious divergence between Christianity and Islam than is found even on the question of divine unity. In my experience of teaching Christian theology and Islamic theology, I find that the doctrines of original sin and redemption are the elements of Christian faith that Muslims find most inexplicable, gratuitous, and even blasphemous in their implication. Nevertheless, the universal human condition obviously offers opportunity for interreligious dialogue that this chapter attempts to explicate.

I should state at the beginning that I will focus on the Sunni-Christian debate with particular leaning towards Roman Catholic theological thought. As Mahmoud Ayoub has shown in his important study, the Shiʻi tradition has always given an important place to redemptive suffering, though not, as he notes, in the Christian sense.[4] The figure of Hussein in Shiʻi piety and that of Christ in the Christian tradition produce fascinating parallels and contrasts but is outside the scope of this chapter.

## Sin in Christian Thought

According to the *Catechism of the Catholic Church* sin is an "offense against reason, truth, and right conscience." Sin is also "an utterance, a deed, or a desire which breaches the eternal law."[5] Sin is considered failure in true love for God and neighbor. It is an offense against God: "Against you, you alone, have I sinned, and done that which is evil in your sight" (Ps 51:4). Sin sets itself against God's love for humanity and as a result turns human hearts away from Him. Thus, it is disobedience, a revolt against God. Sin is, in this way, "love of oneself even to contempt of God."[6] It is also an offense against human nature and damages human solidarity and unity, which is a vital ingredient among individuals with a common interest. The root of sin

3. O'Collins, *Interpreting Jesus*, 141.

4. Ayoub, "Need for Harmony," 15; Ayoub, "Roots of Muslim-Christian Conflict," 42; Ayoub, "Christian-Muslim Dialogue," 66; Ayoub, "Idea of Redemption."

5. *Catechism of the Catholic Church*, 1849.

6. Augustine, *De civitate Dei*, 14, 28.

is in the heart of humans, in their free will, according to the teaching of the Lord (Matt 15:19–20).

The *Catechism of the Catholic Church* makes a distinction between sins: there are mortal and venial sins. A sin is mortal when it damages love (charity) in the heart of human beings or turns a person away from God, who is his or her ultimate end, for an inferior good.[7] Three conditions must come together for a sin to be mortal: the object of the sin must be grave, the sin must be committed with full knowledge, and committed with deliberate consent (Mark 3:5–6; Luke 16:19–31). Sin is deemed venial when, though it allows love (charity) to subsist, it offends and wounds it. Venial sin weakens love (charity). It impedes the soul's progress in the exercise of the virtues and the practice of the moral good. It merits temporal punishment.

Christians believe that sin creates an inclination to sin. It also gives rise to vice by repetition of the same acts.[8] This results in a perverse tendency that blinds the conscience and often corrupts true judgment.

## Sin in Islamic Thought

The doctrine of sin can be defined in Islamic thought as, first and foremost, breaking of the law of God on purpose. It is also wrongdoing of any kind and a violation of any Islamic law or standard, as of taste or propriety. The most dangerous type of sins comprise those grave or deadly sins that are hidden in the heart such as idolatry, atheism, heresy, hypocrisy, envy, malice, vanity, arrogance, conceit, and cheating.[9]

According to Islamic tradition, to commit a sin is human, but to forgive is divine. Though all human beings are created in a pure, natural state (*fitra*), they have a propensity to sin.[10] Islamic teachings state that humans are born naturally good; they have a natural tendency to worship only one God. In Islam, even though humans are born free and pure from any sin, they are still susceptible to sin and held responsible for that after reaching the age of maturity. Since Islam teaches that humans are born naturally good, the concept of divine redemption does not exist in Islam as it does in Christian thinking.[11]

---

7. *Catechism of the Catholic Church*, 1855.

8. Ibid.

9. Rhodes, *10 Things*, 74.

10. Al-Faruqi, *Islam and Other Faiths*, 139.

11. Cf. Ayoub, "Idea of Redemption," 93–94.

Like Christians, Muslims often put sin into two main categories: grave sins and venial sins. Grave sins are offenses that transgress on the rights of God, individuals, and society. All other sins are venial. The categories of sin in Islamic thought were discussed and resolved in relation to the issues of faith and deeds. In the face of serious sins committed by many Muslims, and most particularly by the leaders of the community, (one thinks, for example, of 'Uthman, the third caliph after Muhammad, and his murder in 656 and other caliphal disputes), there arose the question of whether a Muslim guilty of a grave sin (*khati'a*; *ithm*), as distinct from a minor sin (*sayyi'a*), was still a believer.[12]

The issue of the origin of human action, good or bad, generated and continues to generate interesting responses in Islamic thought. A doctrinal sect, the Qadarites, the forerunners of the Mu'tazilites, argued in support of the power (*qadar*) of human beings over their actions, good or bad. The Qadarite position is that human beings alone carry their sins out but are consequently requited for them solely by divine justice. In other words, evil and sin do not come from God but from human beings, under the influence of the devil. Thus, human beings are free and responsible for their actions.[13] Another sect, the Jabarites, believe that the all-powerful God does not only guide and lead astray whom he wills, but also creates faith or unbelief in human hearts, evil or good. God, then, is the sole agent and humans have no control over their actions.[14] However, the Murji'ites are those who refuse to pass judgement on human action and practiced *irja'*, the deferral to God of any judgement on the Muslim who sins. They did not consider deeds, good or bad, relevant to faith.[15]

## Original Sin in Christian Thought

### Development of the Doctrine

A common belief exists among many religious people that a person is flawed even before he or she has chosen to sin. It is also believed that the human being belongs to a race that has suffered a collective perversion and

12. For more, see chapter 8.

13. Watt, *Formative Period*, 94. See also Casper, *Historical Introduction*, 154.

14. Casper, *Historical Introduction*, 155

15. Watt, *Formative Period*, 119.

a fall from moral integrity. In our personal experiences we are constantly aware of a force that pulls us down from our ideals.

Various religious traditions have attempted to explain this human inclination to sin in many ways. For many Christians, especially those in Western traditions, the response to this human inclination to sin is found in the doctrine of "original sin." This doctrine claims that God endowed the first human beings (Adam and Eve) with privileges that their descendants were to inherit. These privileges essentially included a life in free submission to God and the gravitation to the good upheld by God's law. They were also neither liable to death, nor toil and pain, and even wickedness. But Adam and Eve not only lost these privileges for themselves when they sinned, but also for their descendants. They, and we, their successors, like them, became liable to pain, toil, and death (Gen 3:16–19). Humanity forfeited that moral equilibrium, the propensity to submit to and to live in good relationship with God that was the original endowment of the human race.[16]

The emergence and initial development of the idea of original sin are found in reflections of bishops and theologians during the Christian church's first four centuries.[17] The theology of original sin, it must be noted, developed incrementally in the writings of the church fathers. Early church fathers such as Tertullian (d. 220) and Origen (d. 299) often refer to the first sin as "Adam's sin" in their writings. Augustine of Hippo (d. 430) is credited with introducing the idea of inheritance into the discourse on the meaning of original sin. He also took fragments of the idea of original sin in the scriptures and in the writings of earlier church fathers and used them as evidence of divine truth revealed to the church. Later, the church councils of Carthage (418) and Orange (529) made the idea of original sin an essential component of the Western church's doctrinal tradition.[18]

## Soteriological Concerns of Original Sin

At the core of the concept of original sin is a soteriological concern, namely, the firm belief that Christ had overcome the estrangement of humanity from God caused by original sin. Through his death and resurrection, Christ reconciled humanity with God and the human race regained the lost original

16. Yarnold, *Theology of Original Sin*, 24.

17. Rondet, *Original Sin*, 37.

18. Wiley, *Original Sin*, 75. On Eastern Christian distinctions, see Ware, *Orthodox Church*, 216–18.

privileges. Though a lot was said about sin in theological discourses, the interest of many church fathers was not primarily with the problem of sin, but with God's remedy to the problem, which is Christ.[19] The idea of an inherited or original sin served as an explanation for why sin is universal, and thus the universal need for redemption.[20]

Medieval theologians in the West generally accepted the doctrine of original sin without question. Thus, the doctrine continued to assume a core component of divine truths revealed to the church. However, in relation to original sin, medieval theologians preoccupied themselves with issues about human nature itself. Through vigorous speculations, Anselm of Canterbury (d. 1109) and Thomas Aquinas in particular, conceived of two important states of human nature: "before and after Adam's sin." They saw a contrast between the two human states that they described as the "essence of original innocence" and the "essence of original sin."[21] They eventually settled on two spiritual effects of Adam's sin on the human person: first, the loss of original justice, which is a state of sin or guilt, and the absence of sanctifying grace; second, concupiscence and weakening of the will.[22] Medieval theologians further developed stratagems to explain and justify the doctrine of original sin and the necessity of salvation in Christ.

## Ecclesiastical Concerns of Original Sin

Later councils, particularly that of Trent (1545–1563), adopted a perspective that linked concerns of salvation with the ecclesial establishment making the church the only instrument of salvation. The council, which turned out to be one of the Roman Catholic Church's most important councils, was, essentially, prompted by the existing threats to church doctrines stemming from Pelagius (d. c. 418), as well as Martin Luther (d. 1546) and the Protestant Reformation. The council denoted the official definition of the doctrine contained in the decree on original sin passed in the fifth session of the council (1546).[23] Apart from entrenching the relation between original sin and Christ's redemption, the council postulated that human beings need the church in order to secure Christ's forgiveness of Adam's sin.

19. Wiley, *Original Sin*, 54–55.

20. Ibid., 57.

21. John Paul II, *Theology of the Body*, 51–52.

22. Yarnold, *Theology of Original Sin*, 66.

23. Ibid., 67.

## Relational Understanding of Sin and Original Sin

One of the champions of the relational understanding of sin and original sin is Tatha Wiley. In his book *Original Sin*, Wiley acknowledges that the doctrine of original sin is relevant in so far as it describes a general, human disordered condition or reality, which he refers to as the "sustained inauthentic" human nature.[24] In view of this, he makes a striking distinction between authenticity of human nature (pre-fall nature) and inauthenticity of human nature (post-fall nature). His description of the doctrine of original sin as "sustained inauthenticity" of human nature not only explains the human alienation from the divine source but also gives a reason for the personal, persistent human inclination to sin. The "sustained inauthentic" human state engenders massive dehumanization in human communities. It is also the reason human beings destroy their personal relationships, failing and hurting even their loved ones.[25]

Sharing the perspective of Wiley, Joseph Ratzinger (Pope Benedict XVI) acknowledges that Christian theology wrongly refers to this disordered state of human affairs with a misleading and imprecise term: "original sin." He contends that it is difficult for many today to accept original sin as a disordered human condition because they think of sin and guilt solely in personal terms.[26] Rejecting sin as a solely personal anomaly or reality, Ratzinger argues that human beings are relational, and they possess their lives only by way of relationship. To be truly human, Ratzinger contends "means to be related in love." But sin means the damaging or the destruction of "relationality," which gives authentic meaning to human existence. Sin is a rejection of human relationality, a "loss of relationship, a disturbance of relationship, and therefore it cannot be restrict the individual."[27]

## Absence of Original Sin In Islamic Thought

Even though, to a large extent, Muslims recognize that humans are flawed even before they have chosen to sin, they utterly deny the doctrine of original sin as it pertains to the fall of Adam and Eve from heaven. Muslims admit that Adam and Eve broke the command of God, and for that reason,

24. Wiley, *Original Sin*, 207.
25. Ibid., 208.
26. Ratzinger, *"In the Beginning"*, 72.
27. Ibid.

they were evicted from heaven. However, they believe that the sin of Adam and Eve did not alter their nature. Their nature was not tainted with that sin and was not turned to a sinful nature that would lure them to do bad deeds in the future. Adam did not change at all when he was banished; he stayed the same person as he had been in heaven. He remained obedient to God on earth.[28]

Muslims also believe that Adam's sin did not have any negative impact on his offspring. Every human being is born free, pure, and innocent. It is recorded in a Muslim tradition that the Prophet Muhammad said, "No child is born except in a state of natural purity (*fitra*) and then his parent makes him Jewish, Christian, or Magian."[29] This means that, in Islam, all humans are born as a blank book and remain like that until they commit sins and break God's law.

With this in mind, one can argue that Muslims do not accept the doctrine of original sin, and their sacred scripture says that the disobedience of the first parents was their own personal sin for which they were forgiven after they repented. Further, Muslims argue that Adam did not commit a grave sin and support their argument by saying that Adam was a prophet of God, and prophets could not engage in grave sin. Otherwise, they would not be entrusted with a very significant task such as conveying God's message to all His subjects.[30] Therefore, rather than saying that Adam committed a major sin, Muslims say that he only made a mistake through forgetting to adhere to God's command; he atoned for that sin, and his atonement was accepted.[31]

In addition, Muslims have a doctrine of sin, but they believe that humans commit sins because they are weak and forgetful, but not because they have an inherited/original sin nature. According to Islamic teaching, Adam repented of his sin, God forgave him, chose him prophet, and guided him in his ways.[32]

---

28. Rhodes, *10 Things*, 74.

29. Sahih al-Bukhari, 23.138. See https://www.sunnah.com/bukhari/23.

30. Rhodes, *10 Things*, 74.

31. Ibid.

32. Thackston, trans., *Tales of the Prophets*, 59.

## Controversies on Redemption through Christ

As far back as the third century, Origen put forward the redemptive strata-gem theory to explain the link between original sin (the Adam and Eve event) and redemption (the Christ event). The theory posited that the devil had certain rights over humans due to Adam's sin, but Satan was defeated when he wrongly tried to extend the domain of death over the sinless Christ. By his victory over the devil after his crucifixion, Jesus released all those who had previously been held by Satan. Writing on the necessity of redemption by Christ, Anselm of Canterbury also presented the satisfac-tion theory that was based on the maxim that the gravity of offenses is mea-sured by the dignity of the one offended. In the case of human sin against the infinitely great and good God, nothing less than the death of God's own son can make up for the wrong.

Of course, not all Christians supported Anselm's satisfaction theory. Thomas Michel points out that Christians over the centuries have done a disservice to this damaged human reality by overemphasizing Adam's sin in causative and in historical terms.[33] Michel advocates for a descrip-tive interpretation of the doctrine of original sin to refer to the universal human condition, which transcends individuals, cultures, religions, and historical periods.

Similarly, the idea of divine redemption has also troubled Muslims. Al-Tabari pointed out that the redemption theory, instead of glorifying Je-sus, rather glorifies Satan.[34] In his famous letter to Leo III, 'Umar indicated that Christians give too much importance to Satan and rejected the Chris-tian claim that Jesus is the victorious Lord of all mankind.[35] Abu al-Walid al-Baji (d. 1081), a famous Maliki scholar, also considered the Christian concept of redemption to be nonsense. He wondered why Jesus should die to save humanity, arguing that even the devil, in what he achieved, neither went so far as to shed his blood, nor alter his condition, nor assume another corporeal form. He concluded that Jesus' life, according to the Christian conception, was a failure, for He achieved less than Moses, Muhammad, and other prophets did.[36] To Ibn Taymiyya (d. 1328), a renowned Sunni

---

33. Michel, *Muslim Theologian's Response*, 424. See also, Yarnold, *Theology of Original Sin*, 25–32.

34. Gaudeul, *Encounters and Clashes*, 183. See also Gaudeul, *Riposte aux Chretiens*.

35. Gaudeul, "Correspondence."

36. Gaudeul, *Encounters and Clashes*, 182. See also Dunlop, "Christian Mission."

theologian of the Hanbali school of law, the Christian redemption solution was nothing less than blasphemous.[37] He wondered why God would resort to the stratagem of concealing the divine nature in the person of the sinless Christ in order to defeat Satan. And so, to Ibn Taymiyya, the stratagem of Origen imputes deviousness and wickedness to God.[38] Following this line of Muslim thought, Rashid Rida (d. 1935), the Syrian Islamic reformer, also expressed concern about redemption by Christ, claiming that such a notion violated God's justice and concluding that the "claim of the people of the cross, therefore, that clemency and forgiveness are opposed to justice, is unacceptable."[39]

Instead, according to Islamic thought, redemption is found, not through a seeming violation of justice, but in God's perfect justice and mercy. Muslims who follow God's straight path find their way towards Him. On the final Day of Judgement (*Yawm al-Din*), in the Qur'an, Muslims have their good and bad deeds weighed before them by a divine scale (Q 7:8–9; 21:47; 86:9), each one hoping in the boundless mercy of God to find them worthy of Paradise (*Jannah*).[40]

## Conclusion: Common Ground for Christian-Muslim Dialogue

### Personal Sin and Forgiveness

When Christians and Muslims address the question of sin, most often they are referring to personal sin committed by individuals. On this matter, Muslims and Christians find they have much in common. Islam regards sin as a personal act of disobedience and wrongdoing (*zulm*), a spiritual sickness whose primary victim is the sinner. Unless the individual rejects sin and disobedience in sincere repentance, there is no forgiveness and no salvation. This means that salvation comes to the sinner by way of repentance. Christians agree with Muslims that when a person gives oneself over to sin,

---

37. Michel, *Muslim Theologian's Response*, 465.

38. Ibid.

39. As quoted in Ayoub, "Toward an Islamic Christology II," 175.

40. McKane, ed., *Al-Ghazali's Book*, 1–6, 27, 29, 45. See also, Ayoub, "Idea of Redemption." On the unforgivable sin, attributing partners to God (*shirk*), see Waardenburg, *Muslim Perceptions*, 7; McAuliffe *Qur'anic Christians*, 207; and Goddard, *History of Christian-Muslim Relations*, 29.

the proper relationship with God is disrupted. When individuals repent, God generously forgives them and immediately wipes out their personal or subjective guilt. In this sense, both Islam and Christianity preach the ready availability of God's abundant forgiveness that requires sincere repentance as its necessary precondition.

Such shared views notwithstanding, many Christians claim that both forgiveness and redemption are also necessitated by Christ through the instrumentality of the church. Thus, at Trent, the council did not only secure the relation between original sin and Christ's redemption, but also the church. The council asserted that human beings need the church because they require Christ's forgiveness of Adam's sin. In other words, Trent located salvation exclusively in Christ and the church, fostering a dismissal of possibilities of salvation in other religious traditions.[41]

The Christian and ecclesial exclusivism that characterized much of the patristic and medieval doctrine of the church—rooted in the doctrine of original sin—remained dominant in the Roman Catholic Church until the Second Vatican Council. Adopting a christocentric approach, the council fathers toned down the church's earlier exclusivist position and spelt out an inclusivist stance in its documents (*Lumen gentium* and *Nostra aetate*). The council fathers, in the spirit of dialogue, further acknowledged non-Christians as capable of salvation by grace. This means that Jesus dealt with original sin and the sin of all human beings by his death on the cross, rendering human, social, and cultural obstacles of other religious traditions incapable of being a permanent blockage to the grace of Christ for their followers. This grace that emanates from Christ Jesus engages Muslims in their spiritual and material circumstances and offers them the possibility of partaking in the redemption by Christ in a way known only to God.[42]

## Christian-Muslim Cooperation for Mutual Benefits

In relation to the doctrine of original sin, Ratzinger contends that because the network of human relationships is damaged from the very beginning, every human being enters into a world that is marked by relational damage with selfishness and greed as attendant evils. A person begins human existence confronted by a sin-damaged world that often promotes individualism

41. Wiley, *Original Sin*, 208.

42. Second Vatican Council, *Gaudium et spes*, 22; John Paul II, *Redemptoris missio*, 10.

to the detriment of others. Each of us enters into a state of affairs in which "relationality" has been badly hurt. Each person is, from the start, damaged in relationships and does not engage in them as he or she ought.[43]

Consequently, confronted by a common human condition, an inclination to sin and evil as a result of relational damage, Christians and Muslims as individuals and even communities urgently need to embark on various projects to enrich or improve each other for better relationship. This enrichment should not only be in relation to basic tenets of faith and rites of worship, but also with regard to individual spiritual growth. This personal and communal enrichment should begin with a genuine interest in each other, an interest of love that seeks the advancement of the other.

In fact, Christian and Muslim communities have enriched themselves throughout history as they encounter and interact with each other in larger communities.[44] Whenever Christian communities clashed with Muslim communities in history there was always an offshoot—courageous people from both sides who rose beyond the tenets of their particular tradition, and often contrary to the guidance of their spiritual leadership, not only to reach out to the other in the spirit of common brotherhood but also to embrace whatever good they found in their traditions.[45]

## Confronting the Ills of Society Together

Through dialogue, Christians and Muslims can work together to confront the pervasive ills of society that hold humanity back and prevent it from maximizing its relational potentials. Gerald O'Collins identifies three levels of human condition that call for immediate collective response. The first is the menace of death, sin, law, and demonic forces. Forces of evil such as uncontrollable greed, exploitation, institutional injustice, the arms race, revenge attacks, and violence of all kinds abound in the national and international structures of power that dominate the corporate world. The second is the effects of sin and guilt, engendering an impure state for sinful human beings that soils and stains both individuals and even entire nations. The third is the pervasive indifference towards the sufferings of others, rampant fear, failure to forgive, and institutionalized hatred for other races and

---

43. Ratzinger, "In the Beginning", 73.
44. Gaudeul, Encounters and Clashes, 245.
45. Ibid.

religious traditions.[46] These oppressive forces have reached proportions in human societies that demand both individual and communal responses. Christians and Muslims can collaborate to deal with this societal menace.[47]

## Theological Basis for Christian-Muslim Cooperation

Despite belonging to various religious communities, Christians and Muslims have to acknowledge that their individuality is fully expressed not only in their common humanity but also in the common damaged state of affairs they find themselves in.[48] A proverb of the Akan people of Ghana says, "All human beings are children of God; no one is a child of the earth." Similarly, an Akan epigram teaches that, "All belong to one family, though they are separate stalks." To this effect, Kwesi Wiredu notes that human value among the Akan is ". . . intrinsically linked with recognition of the unity of all people, whether or not they are biologically related."[49] In the same way, the unity of humanity applies whether or not we are of diverse religious backgrounds or kinship groups.

This perspective of common humanity is shared by Muslim intellectual Isma'il al-Faruqi in his rendition of "humane universalism." Al-Faruqi argues that "humane universalism," or common humanity, is a fundamental teaching of Islam, which has universal appeal and significance as the most authentic and central issue in the field of interreligious encounters and peaceful co-existence.[50] In fact, it is an offshoot of the concept of *tawhid* that brings all human creatures under the divine authority of the Supreme Deity.[51] Likewise, the Second Vatican Council, in its document *Nostra Aetate*, draws attention to this human connectivity and communality and the need for good relationships among all people irrespective of religious backgrounds: "One is the community of all peoples, one their origin, for

46. O'Collins, *Interpreting Jesus*, 136. See also, Ricoeur, *Symbolism of Evil*, 25–46.

47. Oddbjørn Leirvik acknowledges the concern from some secular liberal communities that Christian-Muslim collaboration could work to promote "conservative positions" that undermine the secularization process, but he also observes the development of an "ethic of civility" that suggests Christians and Muslims may well contribute to the wellbeing of communities. See Leirvik, *Interreligious Studies*, 40–41.

48. Gyekye, *African Cultural Values*, 24.

49. Wiredu, *Cultural Universals and Particulars*, 76.

50. Al-Faruqi, "On the Nature," 129–30.

51. Ibid., 132–34.

God made the whole human race to live over the face of the earth."[52] In Pope Paul VI's document on the church, *Ecclesiam suam*, the Pope notes that the church shares ". . . with the whole of human race a common nature, common life,"[53] and so a common condition.

In these documents the Roman Catholic Church acknowledges the common humanity and condition of all people, touting it as the unique theological foundation for interreligious dialogue, communal harmony, and peaceful co-existence. Common humanity for communal survival is also the framework on which the British Council of Churches set out its guidelines in 1981, "Relations with People of Other Faith," which among other things says, "What makes dialogue between us possible is our common humanity, created in the image of God. We all experience the joys and sorrows of human life."[54] So not only does shared humanity draw Christians and Muslims together in dialogue, but our shared human condition, despite some of our differing theological perspectives, might also bring us together in efforts towards peaceful cooperation.

52. Second Vatican Council, *Nostra Aetate*, 1.

53. Paul VI, *Ecclesiam suam*, 97.

54. The British Council of Churches, now called the Council of Churches in Britain and Ireland, is a subsidiary of the World Council of Churches (WCC). The guidelines quoted here are actually based on the general guidelines provided by WCC. See Davies and Conway, eds., *World Christianity*, 270.

8

# The Formation of Christian and Muslim Communities

## Lucinda Allen Mosher

Community: a social group comprising people with shared characteristics or interests that perceives itself (or is perceived by others) as somehow distinct from society at large. The very notion of religion—the linguistic roots for which lie in words meaning bound together or bound back to those who came before us—implies community. While such a religion-group may be constituted by kinship, creed, initiation, or some combination of these, it will justify itself by means of "identity-giving parameters."[1] In other words, for a community to be perceivable it must have boundaries; the existence of outsiders is presumed.

This investigation of community[2] begins by acknowledging that Christianity and Islam are categories that together account for the religious identity of more than half of humankind presently.[3] As Jamal Elias points

1. McGrath, *Genesis of Doctrine*, 11.

2. My approach to this topic rests firmly on the proceedings of the twelfth annual Building Bridges Seminar (Doha, Qatar, May 2013), for which "The Community of Believers" was the theme for dialogical scripture-study. Thus, I owe quite a debt to my seminar colleagues for many of the ideas herein. Among them, special gratitude is extended to David Marshall and Asma Afsaruddin, whose comments on an early draft strengthened this essay considerably. For the seminar proceedings, see Mosher and Marshall, *Community of Believers*. Thanks go as well to Jonathan Homrighausen, research and proofreading assistant.

3. The Pew Research Center finds that roughly 2.2 billion people identify as Christian (32 percent) and 1.6 as Muslim (23 percent). Pew Research Center, *Global Religious Landscape*.

out, it is "possible to speak of numerous 'fault-lines' of identity along which one can differentiate Muslims, these being lines of language, ethnicity, race, nationhood, gender, attitudes toward the modern world, experience with colonialism, age, economic status, social status, sectarian identity, and so on."[4] Likewise, Christians! We are wise to bring healthy skepticism to the suggestion that *the totality* of adherents to either religion worldwide could be construed as a distinct group with shared interests. Yet both religions, as we shall see, assert an ideal of *oneness*. If cohesiveness indeed be a value, whose notion of "unity" shall obtain? Paradoxically, as Lucy Gardner has pointed out, any commitment to a vision of unity will "almost inevitably (if somewhat perversely) lead to dispute and division," raising questions as to which differences to eradicate, relativize, or accommodate.[5] With all of this in mind, here follows a brief account of ecclesiology and umma-tology: study of theological and other factors that bind Christians (on the one hand) and Muslims (on the other) together, thus of how the nature and purpose of community is construed in each religion; factors leading to each community's fracturing; and approaches each have taken toward maintenance or restoration of unity.

## Constitution, Theology, and Purpose of Community

### Christianity

The biblical term most directly connoting our working definition of community is *ekklesia* (from the Greek for "civic assembly"). *Ekklesia* (and its English equivalent, "church") has several levels of meaning: a group assembled for worship, i.e., a congregation; a company of Jesus-followers (local, regional, national, global) who, as a group, manage their affairs (including worship, education, outreach);[6] or, "all Christians everywhere"—and, in this sense, may include the faithful departed. As used in the New Testament (nearly 120 times) *ekklesia* almost always denotes Jesus-followers as a collective.[7] The authors of the Gospels use the term only rarely. Rather, they

4. Elias, *Islam*, 15.

5. Gardner, "Perspectives on Christian Desires," 49.

6. In this sense, church is as likely to indicate an independent, completely self-sufficient congregation (e.g., the Park Street Bible Fellowship) as a vast network (e.g., the more than seven thousand congregations of the Episcopal Church—which it calls "parishes").

7. The Septuagint (the Greek translation of Jewish scriptures in use during Jesus'

record Jesus' use of numerous metaphors to describe believers collectively or to instruct them as to the sort of group they should aspire to be. The Apostles continue that practice in their epistles.[8] Thus the metaphor "the Body of Christ" quickly becomes and remains a synonym for *ekklesia* (e.g., 1 Cor 12).

In Christian thought, *ekklesia* may be defined as "the body of people who give thanks to God in remembrance of Jesus Christ."[9] Traditionally, its entry-rite is baptism; its defining practice, the sharing of a ritual meal. Regarding the church's essential nature, most Christians would concur it is both fellowship and institution. On the one hand, it is "a spiritual society"—a "mystical and indivisible communion."[10] Through baptism, all its members "are made one in Christ, despite their different origins and backgrounds."[11] Some would call it a sacrament (an outward and visible sign of an inward and spiritual grace). In this vein, the church may be seen as an extension of the Incarnation; that is, the church continues the divine/human unity begun in Christ Jesus.[12]

On the other hand, the church, "the repository of true Christian teaching," is a fellowship—a "school of friendship" with God and neighbors, whose purpose is to enable believers "to grow more Christlike through following and submitting to the call of God, through the power of the Holy Spirit, and through mutual support, prayer, and praise." It enables them to "participate in the life of Christ," experiencing "transfiguration, resurrection, ascension" themselves, and then to share what they have learned.[13] While the Bible is scripture for all Christians, how it functions in this "school of friendship"—how it is studied, interpreted, read in communal worship—varies widely among (and even within) Christian bodies.

---

time, foundational to the Christian Old Testament) also makes frequent use of *ekklesia* as well—most often representing either the Hebrew *qehila* or *qahal*, both from the verbal root Q-H-L (to gather; to summon), and usually to mean a "covenantal body" or an "assembly of the faithful."

8. Paul Minear identifies ninety-six such New Testament images or analogies of "church." See his *Images of the Church*.

9. Morse, *Not Every Spirit*, 315.

10. McGrath, *Introduction to Christianity*, 213; see also Dulles, *Models of the Church*, 15, 47.

11. McGrath, *Introduction to Christianity*, 213, 214.

12. Macquarrie, *Principles of Christian Theology*, 389.

13. See D'Costa, "Nature and Purpose," 3–4; McGrath, *Introduction to Christianity*, 214; Macquarrie, *Principles*, 388.

According to the Nicene Creed—a formula widely used in Christian communal worship—the church is characterized by four "marks": the church is one, holy, catholic, apostolic. The church is *holy*, because God the Holy Spirit dwells in it and acts through it (despite the sinfulness of fallible believers)—its essential purity to be realized in the Last Day. It is *catholic* (from the Greek *katholikos*, "referring to the whole") in that it is universal, beyond any particular time or place. The church is *apostolic*, in that it continues the teaching, practice, and fellowship of the first Christians. Even if they do not use the language of this ancient affirmation of faith, all branches of Christianity see their particular church as embodying these characteristics—but may tender serious concern as to whether such is the case with other Christian denominations or sects.

At the core of apostolic fellowship are two distinctive Christian practices: baptism and the sharing of bread and cup. Baptism is the classic marker of membership in the Christian community. With rare exceptions, Christians understand it as a ritual involving water, which the candidate receives by immersion, pouring, or sprinkling. As for meaning, two understandings prevail. For some branches of Christianity, the action with water actually makes one a Christian; for others, it is an act of obedience publicly acknowledging that one has already become Christian through personal acceptance of salvation in Christ. In the early church, with the bath came access to the Christian ritual meal, the sharing of bread and cup, variously called Eucharist, Holy Communion, or the Lord's Supper. This remains the case in most expressions of Christianity. But again, Christian churches that maintain this custom differ about how often the meal should be held and what it signifies. For some, it is a weekly or even daily act, central to most congregational worship; for others, it is an occasional observance: monthly, quarterly, or even simply annually. For some, it is a reenactment of Christ's once-for-all sacrifice on the cross; for others, it is a memorial service, performed because Jesus told his disciples, "Do this in remembrance of me" (1 Cor 11:24; Luke 22:19); for still others, notions of sacrifice and remembrance are held in dynamic tension in the liturgy; and for others, the ritual is primarily a foretaste of the heavenly banquet yet to come. Christian bodies that officially accept each other's understanding of this meal and right to perform it are said to be "in communion" with one another. For centuries, it has been the case that many Christian branches and denominations are *not* "in communion" with each other—thus calling into question the first "mark" of the church: that it is *one*.

Oneness of the Body of Christ is, therefore, core Christian doctrine. Yet, as Lucy Gardner observes, "the experience of every Christian today is that the church is palpably not in any ordinary sense 'one.'"[14] It is no longer possible, if it ever was, to speak of the oneness of the community of Christian believers, institutionally or sociologically. Since Jesus, on the night before he died, prayed fervently that the community he established during his earthly ministry might "all be one" (John 17:11–26), the church's not-oneness scandalizes and requires a theological explanation. Theological efforts to resolve the "contradiction between a theoretical belief in 'one church' and the brute reality of a plurality of churches," says Alister McGrath, fall into four categories.[15]

First, the imperialist theology asserts the existence of only one true church, only one valid institution. All other claims to be "church" are mere approximations (perhaps fraudulently so). Second, a variant on this is to speak of the church versus "the churches," as does Roman Catholic ecclesiology.[16] In a sense, denominations and movements such as Jehovah's Witnesses, Latter-Day Saints, and some Anabaptist groups can also be said to hold an imperialist ecclesiology: the attitude that only their group expresses the true church.

Third, a Platonic ecclesiology—held by many Protestants—distinguishes between the "invisible communion of believers" (the True Church) and the plethora of "visible churches," the latter being regarded as merely human-made institutions.[17] Rejecting this approach, Christopher Morse asserts that one "cannot speak about the body of Christ without speaking about these bodies of people visibly gathered [for the rite of the Lord's Supper]." The church, he insists, "does not exist apart from some particular human gathering embodied in the material circumstances of a specific location on the corner or down the road even when the mystical communion of that gathering is said to exceed its local boundaries and extend beyond death itself unto the very hosts of heaven."[18]

---

14. Gardner, "Perspectives on Christian Desires," 45–46.

15. McGrath, *Introduction to Christianity,* 215–16.

16. As Gardner points out, many non-Roman Catholics recognize some primacy for the pope in Rome, but will not go so far as to accept Roman Catholic dogma claiming the papal office's universal jurisdiction or infallibility. Gardner, "Perspectives on Christian Desires," 61n33.

17. Dulles, *Models of the Church,* 135.

18. Morse, *Not Every Spirit,* 296.

Fourth, a biological ecclesiology asserts that the church is an organic unity despite differences. Just as a tree has many branches yet remains one tree, so it is with the church.[19] Just as the Son shares unity with the Father in the power of the Spirit, so, says Gardner, the church's "character is of a uniting love that relativizes difference but does not eradicate them."[20] A biological approach may also remind us that Jesus' resurrected body still bears the wounds of crucifixion. The church is one in its brokenness.

Thus, the unity of the church is an ideal toward which many Christians strive, even as they fall into further fragmentation over social, political, and theological issues. Motivating them is the eschatological dimension of the church's oneness. Since the New Testament vision of ecclesial oneness "is properly the unity and communion of the whole world having been transformed and even re-created," the church, while now an earthly institution, can only come fully into being at the Last Day.[21] Therefore, Christians pray regularly that "all may be one;" they sing hymns expressing hope for the cessation of divisions; and in various ways they affirm a oneness that is simultaneously "already" and "not yet."

## Islam

In Islam, the term paralleling *ekklesia* in the sense of "a group assembled for worship" is *jami'a* (a gathering or congregation); the linguistically related *jama'a* (assembly) may also play this role, or may capture the more expanded sense of a company of Muslims who, as a group, manage their affairs (including worship, educational outreach). However, the qur'anic term best conveying our working definition of community is *umma*. It occurs more than sixty times in the Qur'an, almost always in suras from the Meccan period. Linguistically, it may derive from the Arabic *umm* (mother) or *imam* (leader)—or even from Aramaic or Hebrew roots. Whatever its source, the Qur'an uses *umma* in many senses; it can denote, among other things, followers of a particular religion (Q 5:48); the followers of prophets (Q 10:47); the beliefs of a particular group (Q 43:22); a group of people (Q 28:23); a misguided group of people generally (Q 43:33) or among the followers of a prophet (Q 27:83); a period of time (Q 11:8); or even a group

19. McGrath, *Introduction to Christianity*, 216.

20. Gardner, "Perspectives on Christian Desires," 48.

21. Ibid., 49.

of nonhuman beings—such as birds or land animals (Q 6:38).[22] Of high importance is the Qur'an's use of *umma* to designate a righteous contingent within a larger community—as *umma wasat* (middle; Q 2:143); or *umma muqtasdida* (balanced; Q 5:66); or *umma qa'ima* (upright; Q 3:114–115).[23] Major English interpretations of the Qur'an render *umma* variously as "nation," "a [single] people," or "community."

Islam invites membership in a community for Muslims founded on a doctrinal allegiance. The profession of faith that confers membership in that community is the *shahada* (testimony)—that is, formal "attestation to the Unicity (*tawhid*) of God and the historical fact of the communication from God of the Qur'an to Muhammad," as Shahab Ahmed puts it.[24] To say the *shahada* with proper intention is to accept or acknowledge membership in the *umma*. It is built into the daily prayer ritual, which means that pious Muslims reaffirm it many times every day. Some scholars insist, to the contrary, that the *umma* is constituted, not by *shahada* alone, but by embrace and performance of the five pillars of practice: *salat* (five-times-daily ritual prayer), the Ramadan fast, the Hajj, and *zakat* (return of a portion of one's wealth to the community)—plus the aforementioned *shahada*. Ahmet Karamustafa argues sharply against this, noting that "there have been and continue to be millions of people who wholeheartedly adhere to the *shahada* but who do *not* perform [the other four pillars]. Not only that: a good percentage of such Muslims would *not* agree that these four rituals are necessary to be considered a Muslim."[25]

Whatever be the necessity of ritual, Ahmed stresses that is hard to overemphasize the existence of a notion "universally held and experienced among Muslims, that each of them, as an individual *local* Muslim . . . is simultaneously a member of a *universal community* (i.e., human corpus) of *Muslims*." As he goes on to explain:

> This Muslim community . . . is constituted in the self-consciousness
> of each Muslim by the held and experienced fact that all of its members
> bers share a *somehow* or a *something* called Islam—whatever that

22. Saeed, "Nature and Purpose," 15–16.

23. For thorough explanations, see Afsaruddin, "Hermeneutics of Inter-Faith Relations"; and Afsaruddin, "'Upright Community.'"

24. Ahmed, *What Is Islam?*, 137.

25. Karamustafa mentions the Alevi (Turkey), 'Alawi (Syria), Isma'ili, Yazidi, some Shi'i, plus "the millions who choose to emphasize beliefs over acts and consequently de-value the performance of some or all of the four ritualistic pillars." Karamustafa, "Islam," 109.

may be or mean to each one of them . . . [and] no matter how vast, differentiated or contested that domain of meaning might be . . . .[26]

Furthermore, he says, not only do Muslims possess "'a sense of universal human solidarity' across geographical space," they also possess "'a sense of connectedness' across historical time."[27]

If the pivotal concern for Christians in establishing and maintaining unity of the community has centered historically on theological matters, for Muslims, it had most to do with matters of authenticity of leadership. The unity of the nascent Muslim community depended upon political leadership, which the Prophet Muhammad provided. After its migration from Mecca to Medina in 622, that community gained more structure. The so-called Constitution of Medina (also 622) helped to define it,[28] as did the Prophet's Farewell Sermon (632). Shared ritual practice reinforced the nascent community's cohesion; "socioeconomic bonds" enabled its independence.[29] Islam's concept of *umma* took shape gradually. In the Meccan and early Medinan periods, it had scant political dimensions; its usage was broad, thus anyone who believed in God. However, from the mid-Medinan period onward, the term came to be understood more narrowly as referring to the community of the Prophet Muhammad—that is, as one "with its own shared beliefs, understandings, rituals, and eventually its own institutions."[30] In fact, foundational to *umma* as an Islamic concept is its transformative aspect: its ability to play a significant role in making disparate tribes into a community of believers in Islam that transcended ethnic and tribal affiliation.[31] As Islam expanded its domain during the thirty years following Muhammad's death (the era of the Rightly Guided Caliphs, in Sunni perspective), the term *umma* acquired more political characteristics, coming to indicate "a religious and a political community . . . unconnected to any particular ethnicity or geographical location,"[32] thus providing a strong "framework for maintaining religious unity and accommodating the cultural diversities of the believers."[33]

26. Ahmed, *What Is Islam?*, 141.

27. Ibid., 141–42.

28. See Denny, "*Ummah*."

29. Hamza, "Unity and Disunity," 65.

30. Saeed, "Nature and Purpose," 17.

31. Hassan, "Globalisation's Challenge," 312.

32. Saeed, "Nature and Purpose," 17.

33. Hassan, "Globalisation's Challenge," 312.

Over time, the purpose of the *umma* has received much scholarly attention. For Muhammad Asad, its purpose is "to champion justice and fairness, even to the point of violent struggle."[34] For Sayyid Abul A'la Mawdudi, it is to perfect and further the Prophet's mission conceptually and practically, by providing global religious leadership that sets the standard for the middle way, with regard to "social, political and economic ideals, values, traditions and principles."[35] For Sayyid Qutb, who insisted that the term denoted "Muslims only," the *umma*'s purpose is the collective enactment of its members' shared faith.[36] His "conception of the *umma* and its purpose is strictly tied to his broader political project, which is a response to the fragmented society." Thus, it has revolutionary potential.[37]

In both the classical and modern periods of qur'anic interpretation, Saeed notes, we find emphasis on the notion of the community of the Prophet Muhammad as "the best possible"—to the extent that it maintains faith in God, ensures justice and equity, commands the good, and forbids the evil. The classical commentators, happy as they were to take these functions of the *umma* as straightforward in meaning, concentrated their commentary on religious rather than political applications. The modern period, by contrast, Saeed observes, has seen "more debate on the purpose of the *ummah* in terms of upholding justice within an increasingly complex social and political context." In short, *umma* is "a concept that has transformed over time and continues to change as social and political contexts change."[38]

Is the *umma* "one," as Ahmed argues? In some senses, yes. Anthropologist Gabriele Marranci notes that, in the twenty-first century, "the Umma becomes visible and 'activated' in its 'trans-ethnic' and 'trans-national' ethos during particular emotional events," thus overriding various forms of sectarianism.[39] It is also the case that, in contexts where Muslims have felt increasingly disempowered or minoritized, sectarianism becomes a luxury easily overridden.

34. Saeed, "Nature and Purpose," 22.

35. Mawdudi, *Towards Understanding the Qur'an*, 1:19. See also Saeed, "Nature and Purpose," 22.

36. See Afsaruddin, "Hermeneutics of Inter-Faith Relations," 338–39.

37. Saeed, "Nature and Purpose," 23.

38. Ibid., 25.

39. Marranci, *Anthropology of Islam*, 112. As examples, Marranci mentions the Salman Rushdie and Danish cartoon controversies.

## Breaches in Community, Efforts at Healing

### Church

Theologically at least, the church—the Body of Christ—is meant to be "one." The oneness of the Body of Christ does, of course, allow for "churches"— i.e., a multiplicity of local congregations. Multiplicity is acceptable, but not division. A major theme of the New Testament Epistles is, therefore, the need to curb divisive behaviors—such as jealousy, rivalry, bickering—in fledgling congregations.[40] That need remains. As any account of Christian history will emphasize, particularly since (but not solely because of) the advent of Protestantism, the increase in expressions of Christianity has been exponential and unabated; and division caused by "a plurality of rival and conflicting denominations that reject one another's doctrines, ministries, or sacraments" remains unresolved.[41]

Church divisions and efforts to preserve unity are often rehearsed as mostly related to doctrinal disagreements—particularly with regard to Incarnation, Trinity, and soteriology. However, disagreements have also had to do with how the church's oneness, holiness, catholicity, and apostolicity are to be understood and manifested; and regarding polity, how and by whom decisions on faith and order are to be made. The struggles between orthodoxy and Montanism, Marcionism, Arianism, and Donatism are cases in point. Furthermore, such ecclesial divisions and efforts to preserve church unity have never been solely theological or pastoral concerns; always, they have been intertwined with broader cultural and political controversies.[42]

The conciliar approach to resolving breaches in community has long been a Christian strategy. The Council of Jerusalem, described in Acts 15, provides an early example. With that as a model, seven councils were held between 325 and 787. Called "ecumenical" (from the Greek *oikoumene* for "the whole inhabited world"), these were construed as meetings of the "undivided church"—the "whole world" of Christianity—for the purpose of establishing consensus. Each was called to clarify some particular theological matter; but, as Gardner explains, since Ecumenical Councils were intended

40. For an account of the many forms of Christianity extant during the first centuries after Jesus, see Ehrman, *Lost Christianities*. See also Chadwick, *Early Church*.

41. Dulles, *Models of the Church*, 131.

42. Gardner, "Perspectives on Christian Desires," 50. For a succinct summary of what was at stake in each of these controversies, see ibid., 49–52. See also Chadwick, *Early Church*.

as "a means of establishing (or maintaining) peace and good order, including *clear borders*," their decisions also had imperial-political ramifications. Since the consequence for refusal to concur was not just excommunication, but also exile—as was the case with the Council of Nicaea—Ecumenical Council decisions tended to exaggerate, rather than to placate, geographical differences. In turn, this nudged the church toward formal division.[43]

The story of Christianity's struggle for unity may be told in several ways, Gardner notes: as, quite simply "the triumph of truth over heresy"; as the triumph of the power-elite at the expense of all who thought or practiced differently; or as the story of a community gradually coming to terms with itself. Interestingly, perhaps paradoxically, no matter how one interprets the process, the clear cost of any semblance of unity of the Body of Christ is division: century by century, as some sub-groups realize unanimity, "others are excluded, often ultimately along geographical lines"; while certain forms of Christianity take root, some versions "die off as sects or become completely different religions, others to persist as somewhat separate, autonomous, heterodox . . . churches."[44]

However clearly and emphatically they be pronounced and enforced, conciliar decisions never erase competing beliefs or practices. In Italy, for example, Arian Christianity thrived side-by-side with "orthodox" Christianity in the city of Ravenna for several centuries after the Councils of Nicaea (325) and Constantinople (381). Furthermore, a range of Christological positions (and several polities) informed the complexity of Middle Eastern Christianity in the centuries following the Councils of Nicaea, Constantinople, and Chalcedon. When Islam emerged in Arabia in the early 600s, then spread into the Middle East and beyond during the 700s and 800s, it made itself at home in a multilingual Christian milieu. Greek, Syriac, Coptic, Latin, Armenian, and Ethiopic-speaking Christians of that era included Nestorians, Jacobites, and Melkites.[45] This is but one chapter of the story. As the academic field of World Christianity is helping us to understand, the causes of this religion's complexity are many.[46] We can now point to examples of Christian communities on every continent, save

43. Gardner, "Perspectives on Christian Desires," 51; emphasis added.

44. Ibid., 52.

45. See Griffith, *Church in the Shadow*.

46. For comprehensive texts providing this perspective, see Hastings, ed., *World History of Christianity*; and Farhadian, ed., *Introducing World Christianity*, which takes a multi-disciplinary approach and is organized regionally beginning with Africa.

Antarctica, that have developed in isolation from or in contradistinction to conciliar Christianity, each "with their own sets of texts and idiosyncratic liturgies and theology."[47]

A breach of profound significance is the Great Schism—often pinned to the excommunication of the Pope in Rome and the Patriarch of Constantinople, each by the other, in 1054, but in truth the result of many factors. Beyond the political rivalry and experiences between Rome and Constantinople, causes included embrace by the Orthodox and Roman Catholic branches of distinctive and somewhat contrasting understandings of the Four Marks of the church, plus differences in devotional practices, in understanding and use of iconography, in language, and in attitude toward translation of the liturgy.

The Reformation is likewise better understood, not as a single event, but as four streams of reform: Lutheran, Calvinist, Anabaptist, and Anglican. The response to Reformers' critique and demands, while meant to quash divisiveness, actually brought about the formalization of division. With the Reformers no longer "within" the Roman Catholic Church, yet still considering themselves to be Christian, new congregations—and in fact, new communions—were established. With these developments came a spectrum of sometimes irreconcilable interpretations of what is meant by apostolicity and what shall constitute unity.

No matter how the story of the church's struggle for oneness be told by one group of Christians, some others will always feel the need to put forth a counter-narrative.[48] But one thing is sure—and Avery Dulles puts it well; "The present denominational divisions among the churches, in great part, no longer correspond with the real issues that respectively unite and divide Christians of our day. The debates that separated the churches in 1054 and 1520, while they may be revived in contemporary controversy, are no longer the really burning issues."[49] Yet, the belief persists among Christians, if perversely, that they *should* be one—and that Jesus' followers should make concerted efforts toward that end.[50] Foundational to the work of formal ecumenism was an 1870 essay by William Reed Huntington, articulating four essentials to the Anglican Communion's willingness to entertain ecumenical relations with other Christian branches and denominations.

47. Gardner, "Perspectives on Christian Desires," 60n27.

48. Ibid., 45.

49. Dulles, *Models of the Church*, 189.

50. Gardner, "Perspectives on Christian Desires," 45–46.

Now known as the Chicago-Lambeth Quadrilateral, this paradigm calls for affirmation of the Holy Scriptures as containing all things necessary to salvation; affirmation that the historic Creeds (Apostles' and Nicene) are sufficient statements of Christian faith; practice of the sacraments of baptism and Holy Communion; and maintenance of the historic episcopate, locally adapted. On such bases, numerous bilateral dialogues have ensued. In the US, one result has been the establishment of a "full communion" relationship between The Episcopal Church and the Evangelical Lutheran Church in America. The mid-twentieth century saw the ripening of ecumenical efforts: the founding of the World Council of Churches (1948) and the National Council of Churches of Christ in the USA (1950);[51] and the promulgation of several documents crafted by the Second Vatican Council, putting forth a more openhearted notion of the validity of expressions of Christianity outside the Roman Catholic Church.

Be these efforts as they may, achievement of full, visible unity of the church seems never to draw closer. Healing the breaches in community—a Christian enterprise almost since the beginning—gets no easier with the passage of time. Real barriers persist. Perhaps this is the case, Gardner suggests, because, just as the body of Jesus, though resurrected, is still wounded, so it shall ever be with the Body of Christ, the church. [52]

## Umma

That the *umma* is "one" is an oft-repeated lesson of the Qur'an (e.g., Q 3:105). Nevertheless, since early in its history, the *umma* has suffered many fissures; Islam is not unaffected by sectarianism. Most estimates suggest that 85 percent of present-day Muslims are Sunni; some 10 percent are Shi'i; the remaining 5 percent comprises adherents of other sects and Muslims who eschew sectarianism altogether. As with Christianity, efforts to maintain or re-establish unity have, perversely, led to multiplicity. Just as Christianity's Great Schism is best understood as the result of a gradual process involving many factors, so too with the divide between *Ahl al-Sunna wa'l-Jama'a* (People of the [Prophet's] Example and Congregation) and *Shi'atu 'Ali* (the Party of 'Ali)—also known as *Ahl al-Bayt* (People of the House [of the Prophet]). Today's two major streams of Islam (Sunnism and Shi'ism) have

---

51. Each is a fellowship of Christian branches and denominations, but neither of them entirely comprehensive of Christian diversity.

52. Gardner, "Perspectives on Christian Desires," 57.

resulted from distinctive collective memories of formative events—which, in turn, inform their understanding of the transmission and nature of authentic and authoritative leadership of the community of Muslims after the death of the Prophet Muhammad in 632.

Suffice it to say that, during the early post-Prophetic years, communal oneness was strained by what came to be known as the Wars of Apostasy (632–633): tribal rebellions that had at least as much to do with contested political and fiscal authority as with disagreement over theological or religious matters. The *umma*'s first major schism occurred during 'Ali's tenure as the Prophet's fourth Caliph, and was wrought by the Khawarij (literally, "those who walked out"—i.e., secessionists), who disapproved on theological grounds of 'Ali's willingness to resort to arbitration to resolve a challenge to his authority. In offering a competing concept of community and leadership, this schismatic movement brought to the fore the question of whether someone who had committed a serious religious offense could still be "Muslim."[53]

As we have seen, while a timeline may make it seem as though a schism takes place at a definite historical moment and is instigated by a particular event, in reality, the historian's perspective plots it as the result of a multivariable process during which a fissure becomes a canyon-sized breach. Thus, Islam's second major schism, the Sunni-Shi'i divide, rooted in dissatisfaction over the investiture of Abu-Bakr (rather than 'Ali) as the first post-Prophetic leader of the community, was in fact many more generations in the making. A particular account of Muhammad's intentions for leadership after his death informs the Shi'i meta-narrative and doctrine of the imamate that, in its conferral of unique status on 'Ali and his descendants, has soteriological implications. That meta-narrative is also shaped by recollection of the death of Husayn (son of 'Ali; grandson of the Prophet) and the decisive defeat of his followers at the Battle of Karbala, during the armed struggle for control of the caliphate, in 680. While all Muslims see that massacre as a great tragedy, Shi'is see themselves as its remnant. Their distinct devotional practices reflect this.

Over time, Shi'ism has developed its own internal complexity. Since they do not believe that the first three successors to the Prophet's political leadership were legitimate, Shi'is speak, not of four "Rightly Guided Caliphs," but rather, of a series of divinely appointed, infallible Imams. Shi'i

53. For an account of this and other matters in this section, see Afsaruddin, *First Muslims.*

sects differ as to their number and identity. Ithna-'ashariyya (Twelvers)—the majority—believe that there were twelve such inspired leaders. Isma'iliyya (Seveners) differ with Twelvers as to the identity of the seventh Imam.[54] Their Imam for the present day is the Agha Khan. Zaydis (Fivers), prominent in Yemen since the ninth century, are adamant that leaders of the *umma* must be descendants of the Prophet through his daughter, Fatima. Therefore, they see her great-grandson Zayd bin 'Ali as the fifth inspired Imam (rather than Muhammad al-Baqir, whom Twelvers acknowledge).

In spite of the Khawarij and the Shi'i schisms, the oneness of the *umma* remained a priority for some Muslims. Hence the emergence of the Murji'a ("those who suspend judgment")—an emphatically anti-sectarian movement whose principles would lay the groundwork for Sunnism as the community of all who accepted the authenticity of the four Rightly Guided Caliphs.[55] With solidarity as its priority, it reconceived leadership: authority would now reside in the Hadith, the record of the Prophet's example. Leadership would be differentiated, with separate roles for political office-holders and the scholarly class of legal interpreters. According to a saying of the Prophet, "in difference there is mercy." The genius of this solution was its offer of a form of Islamic comprehensiveness—a means for holding "difference" together. Thus, the Sunni notion of the oneness of the *umma* countenances alignment with any *madhhab* (school of legal thought) among the four that long have been deemed canonical.

Given the importance of Hadith in Islamic jurisprudence, *whose* reports of the Prophet's example the community shall follow becomes a crucial question—and on the answer, Shi'is disagree with Sunnis. Therefore, they rely on different Hadith collections. They also differ on the matter of *ijtihad* (independent legal reasoning). Most Sunnis say that the door of *ijtihad* closed centuries ago; now, legal decisions must be made by reference to classical case law. Shi'is, to the contrary, believe it has always been open; thus there is an ongoing role for the *Mujtahid* (literally, striver; expert in independent legal reasoning)—an office not recognized by Sunnis. Such factors have led to differences among Sunnis, among Shi'is, and between Sunnis and Shi'is, on various details of belief and practice.

54. For Isma'iliyya, the seventh Imam was Isma'il (the eldest son of Ja'far al-Sadiq—the sixth Imam), whereas for Twelvers, the seventh was Musa al-Kazim (a younger son of Ja'far).

55. Afsaruddin, *First Muslims*, 57.

While we have already noted Shi'i theology's unique aspects or emphases, the two streams of Islam concur on essentials. At the core of Islamic theological debates has always been *tawhid* (the doctrine of God's absolute oneness), its implications, and how to uphold it philosophically. The Mu'tazila ("those who stand aloof") asserted the createdness of the Qur'an, the necessity of metaphorical understanding of Qur'an passages affirming God's attributes, and the provision by God of human free will. In response, the Ash'ariyya put forth a doctrine of divine foreknowledge that leaves almost no room for human free will. Somewhat midway between these two came the Maturidi position. Ash'arism has long stood as orthodox Sunni theology—a strong unifying element. Neither the Mu'tazila nor the Maturidi have vanished entirely, however.

In recent centuries, more fissures in the *umma* have been caused, frequently by movements determined to reform it. Salafism refers to various austere, even extreme efforts dating primarily from eighteenth-century Arabia. Wahhabism, while sometimes described as a Salafist reform within the Hanbali jurisprudential tradition, has been characterized by Hamid Algar as "a separate school of thought or even . . . a sect of its own," outside the parameters of Sunnism.[56] Three prominent movements arose from the Indian subcontinent. The first, *Ahl al-Hadith* (People of the Tradition), embraces the Zahiri school of legal reasoning that rejects decision-making on the basis of case law. The second, the Deobandi movement (with roots in the Hanafi tradition) rejects eclecticism in jurisprudence. The third, the Ahmadiyya Movement, is distinguished by a theology so unique that, though its followers insist they are Muslim, the mainline deems them heretical.[57] Be that as it may, in the late-1800s and early-1900s, Ahmadiyya were responsible for massive projects involving the translation and publication of the Qur'an and other Islamic literature—resources that were put to broad use.

Further complicating the *umma* is the prominence in North America of several "Islam-based New Religious Movements," analyzed by Judith Weisenfeld as exemplars of "religio-racial identity self-fashioning."[58] Among them are Moorish Science (founded in the early-1900s by Noble Drew Ali) and the better-known Nation of Islam (founded in the 1930s

56. Algar, *Wahhabism*, 2, 3.

57. In 1889, Ghulam Ahmad announced that he himself was the long-awaited Mahdi. Critics say he claimed to be a prophet; most followers deny this. Among their beliefs is the notion that, when someone replaced Jesus on the cross, Jesus was not taken immediately to heaven, but rather, lived on and continued his work in Kashmir.

58. Weisenfeld, *New World A-Coming*.

by Wali Fard Muhammad). Both have propagated teachings irreconcilable with, and worship-practices distinct from, mainstream Islam. While each has moved closer to Sunnism, most Sunnis would not consider them entirely within the *umma*'s boundaries.[59]

Complexification of the unity of the *umma* comes also from Sufism (Islamic mysticism). Sufi orders—many of them transnational—are numerous; at the local level, a Sufi congregation can be close-knit and familial. Some Muslims see Sufism simply as a dimension of normative Islam;[60] some insist on foregrounding their identity as Sufis; others are quite dismissive of it. Further complications ensue from the existence, on the one hand, of movements calling themselves "Sufi"—but having no Islamic content—and, on the other hand, of Muslims whose practices and outlook seem "Sufi" in every way, yet eschew that label.[61]

Clearly, Muslims worldwide are diverse. Yet, as with Christianity, there persists the feeling that Muslims should be "one." The late-nineteenth and early-twentieth centuries birthed some pan-Islamic movements; but so deeply ingrained was the sectarian divide, Feras Hamza notes, that they were "momentarily ecumenical" at best. In the twentieth and early-twenty-first centuries, the term *umma* gained new prominence in Muslim discourse, he notes, but in relation to nationalism for the most part, "as a concept of the imaginary, undoubtedly intended as a socially binding concept existing in a somewhat tense, or at least undefined, relationship to *nationalism*."[62]

With this in mind, we turn our attention to the Amman Message—the most significant effort at Islamic ecumenism in recent decades, perhaps ever.[63] Issued in 2004 in response to Muslim-on-Muslim strife, and then ratified and endorsed by some 500 scholars, it was promulgated as the consensus of the *umma* and is meant as the official legal answer to three questions: who is a Muslim, who has the authority to issue a *fatwa*, and whether declaring someone an apostate is permissible.

Broadly inclusive in its answer, the Amman Message affirms that Muslims may *indeed* differ among themselves on sectarian, jurisprudential, and

---

59. For an introduction to these and several other movements, see McCloud, *African American Islam*.

60. See Murata and Chittick, *Vision of Islam*; Salem, *Emergence*.

61. Nursi, "Sixteenth Letter," 85; Vahide, *Islam in Modern Turkey*, 223.

62. Cf. Hamza, "Unity and Disunity," 74. See also Anderson, *Imagined Communities*.

63. The most thorough account in English of the content and significance of the Amman Message is Hardy et al., *Muslim Identity*.

theological bases. It then asserts that an adherent of *any* of eight schools of jurisprudence—the four Sunni schools (Hanafi, Maliki, Shafiʿi, and Hanbali), the two Shiʿi (Jaʿfari and Zaydi), the ʿIbadi, or the (often controversial) Zahiri—is indeed a Muslim; so are those who subscribe to the Ashʿari creed (traditional Islamic Theology), or who practice what it calls "real" Sufism, or who subscribe to "true" Salafism.

Conciliar statements have their place. However, their trickle-down or ripple-out effect is not always apparent. The Amman Message was a diplomatic document meant to mitigate violent extremism;[64] yet, sadly, notes Jamal al-Shalabi, in the years since its promulgation, "*the tendency towards extremism has increased* [among Muslims]. Moreover, the range of terrorism adopted by the Salafist trend as represented by al-Qaida, Daesh, and the Al-Nusra Front has also increased."[65] Witness also the understandable tendency, when Muslim individuals or groups do something heinous, for the mainstream to say of them, "They are not legitimate Muslims." Attempts to expand boundaries, paradoxically, provoke disunity. Yet, whether buoyed by top-down initiatives (of which the Amman Message is exemplary) or simply drawing upon grassroots initiatives, Islamic ecumenism persists. In North America, it has sometimes taken the form of deliberately pan-sectarian Islamic Centers—institutions built and administered by members of both major streams of Islam—or pan-Islamic activist organizations such as Islamic Networks Group (ING), which includes Sunni, Shiʿi, and Ahmadi Muslims in its Islamic Speakers Bureau.[66]

## Conclusion

Is there now—indeed, has there ever been—a global Muslim community? A global Christian community? No. For both religions, divisions are "born of many types of difference, on many different levels," with regard to a range of issues. Thus, the search for unity will likewise be complex.[67] Undaunted, many Christians continue in ecumenical pursuits; institutionally, many Christian branches and denominations have invested considerable resources. Likewise, many Muslims. Witness the Amman Message initiative,

64. Eiedat, "Amman Message," 151, 158.

65. Al-Shalabi, "Amman Message," 144; emphasis his.

66. ING is based in San Jose, California. See https://ing.org.

67. Here I am adapting Lucy Gardner's observations vis-a-vis Christian ecumenism. See Gardner, "Perspectives on Christian Desires," 56.

the remarkable cooperation of Muslims of diverse traditions in issuing the invitation to dialogue known as "A Common Word Between Us and You,"[68] and the existence and efforts of organizations such as Islamic Society of North America. Importantly, under each religion's umbrella, those with a heart for ecumenism may not hold in mind the same notion of unity! Gardner observes that "some look primarily for theological convergence, some look for greater sharing of administration; others look for . . . merely the cessation of hostilities; some are more concerned for the recognition of unity of purpose and shared social engagement on issues of justice, locally and more globally."[69] She is speaking of Christians, but her remarks ring true for Muslims as well.

That said, it is the case that under any religion's umbrella, as Feras Hamza reminds us, community is often more imagined than real, more "prescribed than actualized." Yet, he says, an "imagined community" may be no "less *real* than a physical/political one." Even where the historical record is an account of disunity, there still is much that is true, real, and uniting in Islam's "devotional language, common praxis, and sacred referents." [70] The same can be said for each of Christianity's major branches, if not for the entirety of the religion in its plethora of expressions.

So, indeed, at a phenomenological level, both religions purport an ideal of unity and suffer a reality of disunity. However, in noting this similarity of situations, we must also acknowledge the difference in theological significance of community in Islam and Christianity—a distinction that stems from their foundational accounts of revelation.

How so? Christianity, as we have seen, speaks of Jesus as the very embodiment of revelation. As God's Word enfleshed, Jesus' primary mission is to bring into being a community of followers who would themselves be the bearers of his presence through their indwelling and empowerment by the Spirit. The task of Jesus-followers would, of course, include promulgation of Jesus' teachings; so, in due course, the community wrote accounts of his words and deeds—but, clearly, for early Christians, establishment of the community took priority over creation of scripture. Thus, for Christianity, the relationship of community to scripture is complex and inter-penetrating at the least—a pattern that can likewise be discerned in the story of

68. "A Common Word" was issued October 13, 2007. See http://www.acommon-word.com/.

69. Gardner, "Perspectives on Christian Desires," 56.

70. Hamza, "Unity and Disunity," 75; emphasis added.

Israel and the emergence of Jewish scriptures. In Islam's meta-narrative, by contrast, the sacred history of scripture takes priority over community. The revelatory moment opens with a command to recite. A scripture starts to come into being as Muhammad recites, and around his transmission of God's Words a community is formed. In due time, the community will collect, preserve, teach, interpret scripture; but in core Islamic theological terms, the community does not give birth to scripture; revelation does. For Muslims, the relationship of community to scripture is neither complex nor interpenetrating.

As a result, ecclesiology is a Christian theme of great theological weight; ummatology, less prominently so in Islamic thought. Metaphors and analogies for "church" abound in scripture and beyond; many a book reflects on what the church *is* (particularly, its being an extension of the Incarnation) as well as what it should do. By contrast, in the Qur'an, in the Hadith, or in Islamic thought, use of metaphors and analogies for *umma* is rare, comparatively. Although the *umma* is a theme of vital significance, it is discussed primarily in functional, rather than ontological, terms. That is, emphasis rests less on what it *is* in itself than on what it must *do* in order to obey God.

And high on the must-do list for *umma* and church alike is self-propagation. Both Christianity and Islam are missional religions. That is, both *umma* and church see themselves as communities under God-given mandates to bear witness to truth as they believe they have received it. Accordingly, Muslims are to engage in *da'wa* (issuance of a call/an invitation to submission to God's "way");[71] Christians, in evangelism (sharing of the Good News of divine salvation through Christ Jesus, accounting for their deep and joyous hope, and in the process inviting others to join in discipleship).[72] But, is *da'wa* or evangelism best conducted aggressively or passively (that is, by one's example primarily, using words only if necessary)? On such matters Muslims and Christians differ among themselves. Thus, in the arena of Christian-Muslim comparative theology, a necessary corollary of ecclesiology/ummatology (study of the nature and purpose of the community of believers) is missiology (study of the nature and methodology of

71. Q 16:125, 42:15, and 3:20 are examples where the Qur'an conveys this.

72. For biblical warrants, see Matt 28:19–20; Mark 16:15–16; 1 Pet 3:15, plus numerous verses in the epistles of Paul.

propagation of the religion), which will lead in due course to study of each faith's beloved exemplars and martyrs.[73]

73. For a succinct and interesting comparison of Christian and Muslim missiology, see Munir, "Islam and Franciscanism."

# 9

# Religious Pluralism and Dialogue

## DOUGLAS PRATT

SHAHRAM AKBARZADEN AND SAMINA Yasmeen refer to the "paradigm of coexistence" that influences the pragmatics of political leadership within the Islamic world.[1] Despite some popular (mis)conceptions of Islam as an exclusionary and dominating religion, throughout the world of Islam there have been, and continue to be, many instances of political détente, cultural cooperation, and respect of other religions. As David Thomas states, "Islam has been involved with other faiths throughout the entire fourteen hundred years of its history."[2] Chief among these have been relations with Jews and Christians, and so varying forms of dialogical engagement depending on circumstance and motivation. However, as Hewer notes, in regard to possessing "the Qur'an and the Sunna of Muhammad," Muslims often consider Islam as "the super-highway of God's guidance" in comparison to which "other faiths are at best meandering lanes."[3] Muslim engagement with Christianity has ever involved a measure of the interplay of affinity and inquiry, along with undeniable antipathy. For although, especially in respect of being equated at times with rival empires, these two faiths have engaged with one another in the context of political and military encounters and clashes, in reality negative interactions have by no means comprised the full story. As Hugh Goddard has noted, "the relationship between the two

---

1. Akbarzadeh and Yasmeen, *Islam and the West*, 2.
2. Thomas, "Islam and the Religious Other," 148.
3. Hewer, *Understanding Islam*, 164.

communities has *not* always been antagonistic and confrontational."[4] In part this is because there has never been just one Islam engaging with just one Christianity. Intra-religious plurality has been the persistent underlying reality for each faith. Islam, soon after its historic inception, was marked by rivalry and alternative perspectives producing the great divide of Sunni and Shi'i, and Christianity was already pluriform with the East-West rupture increasingly obvious. For both Christianity and Islam "the bewildering variety of opinion within each community has given rise to the suggestion that perhaps we should no longer speak of Islam and Christianity but rather of Islams and Christianities."[5] Goddard's point is not just structural and sociological, reflecting the manifest fact of internal socio-identity diversity that applies to each religion; it applies also to the variegated range of theological and ideological positions that is found in each religion. This suggests that in the context of actual dialogue between specific Muslims and Christians it may be discovered that, on some key issues and affirmations, there is a degree of conceptual overlap which may be greater than first thought—at least once the accretions of traditional rhetoric and prejudicial posturing are stripped away, and the issues are subject to appropriate critical scrutiny that engages equally both parties to the dialogue. The reality of multiple "Islams" ever contrasts with the presumption of Islam being a monolithic unity.[6] And much the same can be said for Christianity, for example. This chapter explores some elements of religious pluralism and dialogue with respect to Islam and its relations to other faiths, particularly Christianity. I discuss pluralism as a mode of responding to and comprehending the place of religious diversity, or plurality as such, and examine issues to do with dialogue, focusing on select theological issues.

## Religious Pluralism—Responding to Plurality

Plurality is not the same as pluralism. The former denotes the sheer fact of diversity; the latter names one particular response to the fact. Often the two terms are used synonymously to refer to the generic idea of "many-ness" which can be confusing. In reality there is a variety of ways in which any religion responds to or so contends with religious diversity—both within and without. Even in contexts of relative homogeneity, the fact of

4. Goddard, "Christian-Muslim Relations," 13; emphasis added.

5. Goddard, *Christians and Muslims*, 169.

6. Bennett, *Studying Islam*, 50; cf. Tibi, *Islam between Culture and Politics*, 26.

religious plurality—or diversity—has always been the case, to a greater or lesser degree. Responses to the fact tend to be either in terms of inclusivism, where the implicit challenge posed by plurality is vitiated by including any religious other as, in effect, being already accounted for within the singular worldview framework of a religion or cultural heritage, or in terms of exclusivism, that is, denying or in some way setting aside plurality as of no real import. Kate Zebiri points out that "The majority of Muslims, like the majority of Christians, hold an exclusivist view of truth, in that they believe that their religion is true to a degree that others are not."[7] The sociopolitical consequences of hardline exclusivism are all too clear. Exclusivists may be inimical to dialogue, evincing deep skepticism and suspicion, even to the point of regarding co-religionists inclined to interreligious dialogue as treasonous. However, South African Muslim scholar, Farid Esack, speaks of the experience of internal Islamic variety, or intra-Muslim diversity—the co-existence of various expressions and experiences of Islamic identity and practice.[8] And Muslims, whether in the majority or the minority, have long co-existed with peoples of other faiths in a multiplicity of ways.[9]

From earliest days Islam certainly defined and identified itself as other-than other religions, both in respect of polytheistic and pagan Arabia, and also in regards to Judaism and Christianity and any other religion. Islam commenced with an implied inclusivism, then tended to a hardening exclusivism. By contrast, the paradigm of pluralism, which places high value upon variety and difference, endeavors to account positively for plurality.[10] So today the Islamic world is confronted by the challenge of pluralism, or better, plurality, and this is on many fronts. One has to do with the issue of Muslim minorities in Western secular (or nominally Christian) societies. Another has to do with the multifaceted problem of minorities in the Arab world, for example. Here Muslims must contend with some who are both non-Muslim and non-Arab (for example, Armenians); some who are non-Arab Muslim (Kurds, for instance); some who are Arab Muslim dissenters from majority Sunni Islam (for example, Druzes); and then Arab Christians, for whom God (whose Son is Jesus) is called "Allah." Despite an idealized motif that regards a Muslim land as the only proper place for Muslim existence, the facts of history demonstrate a long-standing Muslim

7. Zebiri, *Muslims and Christians*, 175.

8. Esack, *On Being a Muslim.*

9. Roy, *Globalised Islam.*

10. See, for example, Pratt, "Contextual Paradigms."

propensity for co-existence with religious "others;" a form of acceptable pluralism that amounts to a détente with diversity. But it cannot be taken for granted: for today the "recognition of religious diversity makes it imperative on the part of Muslims to accept those who do not belong to their faith as fellow human beings."[11] And Amir Hussain notes the crucial importance of pluralism and interfaith dialogue to Muslims, especially "where Islam is a minority religious tradition . . . . Muslims living in these countries have to articulate their understanding and practice of Islam in the midst of a plurality of belief systems."[12]

Pluralism poses a challenge to both Islam and Christianity, which traditionally have been at great pains to construct their understanding of reality so as to encompass, on their terms, everything within it. Like Judaism, to which they are linked, these are religions of revealed divine truth with the underlying assumption that this truth is a coherent encompassing unity. In respect of the qur'anic injunction that there is "no compulsion in religion" (Q 2:256), Hewer asserts "this must not be taken to mean freedom of religion in the sense that all religions are equal."[13] Islam is not to be imposed; it is offered as the corrective to those who, having once received the true message, are in need of restoration to the right path of belief and practice. To this extent, Islam can be said to manifest an inclusivist paradigm with respect to religious diversity. Yet, Seyyed Hossein Nasr asserts:

> Islam is an inalienable and inseparable part of the Abrahamic family of religions and considers itself to be closely linked with the two monotheistic religions that preceded it. Islam envisages itself the complement of those religions and the final expression of Abrahamic monotheism, confirming the teachings of Judaism and Christianity, but rejecting any form of exclusivism.[14]

To be sure, for Muslims, the "Qur'an and the Prophet lie at the heart of Islamic thought, and they provide not only the main source of attitudes towards other faiths but also the constraint on what is acceptable and what is not."[15] Thomas argues:

11. Alhabshi and Hassan, *Islam and Tolerance*, 5.

12. Hussain, "Muslims, Pluralism," 252.

13. Hewer, *Understanding Islam*, 165.

14. Nasr, *Heart of Islam*, 42.

15. Thomas, "Islam and the Religious Other," 149.

"there has been a general consensus among Muslims who have thought and written about the faiths . . . that Islam stands as the supreme embodiment of God's will in its scripture and the intellectual disciplines that have sought to unfold its meaning, and the well-balanced societies that have been constructed on its teachings. It has therefore tended to judge other faiths, or elements within them, on the point of how they conform to the norms of Islam itself."[16]

Pluralism is undoubtedly problematic although, in recent times, "Muslim scholars have attempted to emphasize the latitude of the Qur'an and Islam, and to search out new possibilities for the relationship between their own and other faiths."[17] Pluralism raises questions concerning traditional views of divine reality and ascriptions of absolutes. Kenneth Cracknell puts the theological issue, the sheer fact of there being a diversity of religions, rather succinctly.[18] If there is but one God, how is it that there are so many religions? Are we caught in a context of perpetual rivalry? Is the only peaceful option that of mute co-existence at the level of mere tolerance? Or are we called to a life of cooperation with people of other religions? A pluralist affirmation poses theological challenges. Yet this may yet prove a fulcrum for dialogue. For diversity within religions, while often downplayed by pundits of respective orthodoxies, reveals an essential truth of religion as being subject to highly variegated and nuanced tropes of interpretation and so to variability of representation, self-understanding, and identity. This is undoubtedly the case for Islam, as with its chief dialogical interlocutors of Judaism and Christianity, and any other religion of revelation for that matter.

Given that "Islam began as a minority tradition in a non-Muslim setting," Hussain notes the vital element of early engagement of Muslims with Christians in Abyssinia for the story of Islam.[19] He writes that the Qur'an contains verses that can be varyingly positive or negative such that the "various strands of the Qur'an can be used both as a bridge-building tool and to justify mutual exclusivisms."[20] Belief in the God who created diversity, and a qur'anic vision of plurality and cooperative relations with others,

16. Ibid., 171.

17. Ibid., 165.

18. Cracknell, *Considering Dialogue.*

19. Hussain, "Muslims, Pluralism," 252.

20. Ibid., 254.

albeit select religious communities, forms part of the Islamic heritage. And, with reference to contemporary Muslim political discourses, Ahmad Moussalli stresses the importance of "ideological and religious arguments" with regard to pluralism.[21] In relation to this, the concepts of equality (*al-musawat*), freedom (*al-hurriyya*) and justice (*al-ʿadl*) are emphasized. Indeed, arguably the Qur'an demonstrates an acceptance of religious plurality as a "primary Islamic disposition, which . . . provides the foundation for plurality."[22] Furthermore, in this recognition "the Qur'an neither confines faith and salvation to Muslims, nor denies faith and salvation to other religions."[23] Today there are both Muslim and Christian intellectuals who promote the way of pluralism—the recognition and affirming acceptance of the religious "other" as valid, worthy of respect, and a potential dialogical interlocutor—both within and between their respective faiths, as well as more broadly. This sets the platform and provides the necessary support for dialogue to occur.

## Dialogue

Religious pluralism and dialogue go together, for without a positive appreciation for diversity and so a measure of respect for religious "others" there can be no dialogue, no relational détente. Furthermore, dialogue has rarely seemed more urgent than in the current climate of the fear-mongering and anti-Islamic rhetoric that constitutes modern-day Islamophobia. Muslims simply living out their lives in the context of everyday interactions within a religiously plural environment engage in a variety of non-intentional dialogues—or, perhaps better, non-dialogical (discursive) relational interactions. Such engagement occurs without any conscious design as such; they simply take place in the "dialogue of life." Beyond that, various intentional interreligious engagements can and do occur. Joint responses to social issues and cooperative actions, premised on shared, or at least compatible, values and perspectives, constitute a planned intentional level of interreligious relating—the "dialogue of action." And occasions wherein interfaith events of a liturgical, meditative/reflective, or otherwise "worshipful" nature are engaged in, they represent the "dialogue of religious experience." Events where scholars and other allied experts from across two or more

21. Moussalli, "Islamic Democracy," 286.

22. Khatab and Bouma, *Democracy in Islam*, 30.

23. Ibid., 31.

religions get together to pursue deep discussion are often referred to as the "dialogue of discourse:" this discursive activity is what the term "dialogue" immediately suggests, but in fact is the most difficult to pursue and really requires a history of relationship being built up by way of the other modalities of dialogue before it can be confidently entered into. On the question of the meaning of dialogue, Charles Kimball remarks:

> Dialogue, by definition, is a conversation, a process of communication through speech. It is a reciprocal relationship in which two or more parties endeavor both to express accurately what they mean and to listen to and respect what the other person says, however different her or his perspective may be. But dialogue is more than an exchange of views. In a fundamental sense, it is a perspective, a stance, an openness. Dialogue represents a way of relating . . . . Ideally, mutuality in dialogue is present in communication, trust, understanding, challenge, growth, and even spiritual development.[24]

Interreligious dialogue, as an intentional and institutionalized activity, rather than a relatively haphazard encounter, is one of the most notable advances that have occurred in the field of religion during the latter half of the twentieth century. Indeed it is, arguably, only in and through such relational activity that the negative consequences of religious diversity, as expressed, for example, in the many violent interactions that have occurred, and are still occurring, in the name of religion can be overcome. Resolving the competitive clash that has so often colored religious interactions is one of the aims of dialogue. For interreligious dialogue to proceed in the hope, if not expectation, of a productive outcome, then the misapprehensions of the past, together with the prejudices of the present, must be addressed in a climate of mutual and reciprocal correction. So, for example, when Christians and Muslims meet in dialogical encounter, each first needs to know that they faithfully represent and thereby empathetically understand the position of the other. In the process, of course, each must be open to correction by the other, and be prepared to engage in an honest self-reflective critique in the light of the dialogue process. A shorthand way of tackling this process is to think in terms of discerning identity: partners in dialogue need to know their own and their partner's identity. Any religious identity is, in part, constructed by the experience of everyday life, of the living out of duties and obligations, of the concrete expression of belief. This

24. Kimball, *Striving Together*, 86.

is eminently so with Islam. The Islamic religious life is given visible and daily expression in terms of the obligations to fulfill the requirements of piety. This active life of faith is summed up in the "five pillars," the divinely required ordinances of duty (*arkan*). But alongside this universal element of Islamic identity sits the particularity of geographic location. If Islam espouses trans-national identity—the transcendent solidarity of the *umma*, given graphic expression in the Hajj—the realities of geographic location or origin, thus ethnicity, also play a significant part.

Undertaking dialogical engagement, at whatever level from mundane daily interaction to the intentional and intellectually demanding, comes neither easily nor naturally. For the most part we are absorbed enough in the business of our everyday lives, and the sustenance of our own families and communities, to be taking the necessary time, and expending the required energy, to engage in some sort of meaningful dialogical relationship with someone from a totally different community. This is a commonplace of human experience and behavior. But in respect of interactions between Islam, or rather specific Muslim communities, and other religions and their communities—not to mention interaction between Islam and secularized Western cultures—then this commonplace needs itself to be challenged. In many contexts the slogan "dialogue or die" is all too real.[25] Dialogical engagement does not occur in a contextual vacuum. Interfaith encounter, while it can have a theoretical and dispassionate dimension, is essentially a grounded relationship within the real world of religio-cultural identity and the vagaries of socio-political dynamics.

Dialogue is a challenge of immense proportions for it requires us to take serious account of the "other." It requires us to be open to the "other," to view the "other" as neighbor and friend. It implies necessarily some measure of pluralism as a grounding context.[26] Whether within the borders of our own community and worldview—where the religious "other" represents various alternative, heterodox, or radical perspectives that challenge from the inside, so to speak—or whether from without, where the "other" represents a wholly alien religion and culture, the essential challenge is the same. It is the challenge of dialogical engagement that encompasses radically different alternatives—the fact of plurality—as legitimate and potentially compatible co-partners in life. To reach the point of acceptance of the legitimacy of the "other" and their perspective—which is at the root

25. See, for example, Swiddler et al., *Death or Dialogue?*
26. For example, see Pratt, "Pluralism and Interreligious Engagement."

of the issue of pluralism—and to rethink our world-view constructs as a consequence, so as to be able to encompass the "other" as potentially compatible at least to the extent of being a legitimate dialogical partner, involves the deep task of grappling with religious pluralism and the encounter of ideological and theological dialogue.

## Theological Dialogue

One of the critical areas of dialogical interaction, especially between Muslims and Christians, is that of theological encounter. This arena is crucial, but it is also exceedingly difficult. Much good interaction and dialogue can take place between Christians and Muslims in respect of other areas of concern—moral, socio-political, economic, ecological—to name but a few.[27] Nevertheless, fundamental beliefs, and critical expressions of faith, which are those things that signal the bedrock of our respective world views, need to be seriously and sensitively addressed, if only because much of how Islam and Christianity pronounce and act upon issues and problems, with respect to both worldly and spiritual matters, comes down to an extension of fundamental principles and the application of basic beliefs. And most often the succinct belief-expressions are treated as badges of identity that are not easily shared. Islam holds an ambiguous view of Christianity. Christian doctrines concerning the Trinity and the divinity of Christ are traditionally viewed "as compromising the unity and transcendence of God."[28] Yet in the Qur'an there is an acknowledged salvific efficacy in Christianity: "they shall have their reward" (Q 2:62, 5:69). Toleration is affirmed, with the injunction that "different religious communities should exist in complete freedom."[29]

Theological dialogue, and in particular the ideological element or dimension inherent in that, constitutes a major arena of dialogical challenge. Here, by way of an example, we may note the manner whereby Islam and Christianity each interrelates historical founder-figure motif and ideological-religious function. If we take, for the sake of illustration, the two respective historical "founder figures"—for Christianity, Jesus; for Islam, Muhammad—we may like to consider how each religion perceives their particular figure in terms of function. This is important because, typically (although arguably falsely), they are contrasted and compared simply on

27. See, for example, Pratt, *Christian Engagement with Islam*.

28. Kimball, *Striving Together*, 46.

29. Ibid.

the basis that they appear, as historical figures, to function as equivalents. But in point of fact the ideological function is different in each case. For Christianity, Jesus functions as *savior*: the motif of *prophet* is secondary to, and indeed subsumed by that. But, even if the function of "savior" is pre-eminent, it is not the *sole* function ascribed to this figure. Jesus functions also as teacher (so the title Rabbi) and as an exemplar of the ways of God (thus the title Son of God), and so, through all this, together with the activities and events that befall him according to the passion narratives of the Gospels (betrayal, trial, crucifixion, resurrection) he functions as the active agent of Divine Will (thus the title or ascription Word or Logos of God). So, in the subsequent Christian perspective the function of the figure is suggestive of divine being inherent to him; hence the lengthy and complex development of Christian doctrine concerning Jesus. An Islamic reading of the Christian account might conclude that, in the Christian record, there is evidence of unique and particular submission to the Will of God: the Gospel records as among Jesus' last words the petition "Not my will be done, but Thine" (Luke 22:42). Indeed an Islamic reading of the Christian record (as opposed to an Islamic reading of the qur'anic record of Jesus) may form a worthwhile dimension of cross-hermeneutical engagement within the context of theological dialogue.

By contrast, the Islamic perspective on Muhammad as the founder figure is unequivocally straightforward: he was a man through whom God gave to the world the message contained in the utterances which he, Muhammad, was commanded to recite. Muhammad was a prophet, first and last. And in the Islamic view he fulfilled that role as none before him had done. But clearly he did more than just that. A close reading of the Islamic account of Muhammad reveals the motif of *exemplar par excellence*: the motif of teacher; the motif of enacting a divine—that is, divinely willed and sanctioned—mission which resulted in the establishment of a theocratic community wherein is proclaimed and promoted the way of a saving faith. Thus, when considering the ideology of function in respect of a comparison of figure, we can detect aspects of a dynamic parallelism operating at one level, yet we can recognize the impact of ideological differentiation that also applies at other levels. By carefully working through the ideological dimension it may be possible to deconstruct the accretions of dogma and hagiography sufficient to find a bedrock of unique function that allows each religion to co-equally affirm and honor the other's central historical figure in a way that has hitherto been impossible to achieve.

Two key issues, or theological "problematics," which lay behind creedal development within Christianity and have continued to this day to be the source of much debate and scholarly activity, need to be addressed in the context of Christian-Muslim dialogue. The first is the problematic of the nature of Christ. The second is the Trinitarian concept of God. Both have to do with, or perhaps express particular aspects of the issue of the unity of the Divine Being. What for Muslims is no issue at all—the priority of *tawhid* is paramount—for Christians has always been a mystery of the Divine Being: in the context of affirming divine Oneness Christian faith asserts, nonetheless, two forms of plurality. The person Jesus of Nazareth was a man through whom God spoke and acted in a particular way; the title of "Christ," which has dominated as the proper name,[30] and thus contributed to the whole context for raising the question of the nature of Jesus as, putatively, both human and divine, first and foremost speaks of the divine function or action that was effected through this human individual. Christological definitions, which are ontological statements, arose as a result of theological reflection and debate. They are just that: definitions. They are constructs of ontological thinking; products of intellectual endeavor; the results of Christian *ijtihad* we might say.

Likewise, the Trinity is an onto-theological explanatory concept. To talk in terms of inner-trinitarian relations constituting the essential life of God, or as fundamentally descriptive of the Divine Being, is arguably to ontologize a symbolic construct that has itself been derived from the diversity of the human experience of God within the Christian context. Distinctiveness of relationship in regard to any one of the three "persons" is distinctiveness of particularity in divine relational activity as such: there is no need to presume any other relational identity is responsible for the particular relational type, even a relational identity "within" God. The Trinitarian names (Father, Son, Holy Spirit) can thus be seen as denoting three spheres or dimensions of divine relational activity. Analogously, Islam's 99 Most Beautiful Names of God are also indicative of various types and sorts of relationships that it is of the nature of Deity to be engaged in. Arguably it would be a category mistake to contrast Trinity with *tawhid* because the latter is the prior or fundamental concept; the former is but one construct expressing the human understanding of the revelatory experience of God-in-relationship. Christianity, in principle, ought to be able to concur with

---

30. So: "Jesus, the Christ" thence "Jesus Christ" and "Christ" as the alternate names for Jesus.

the Muslim affirmation of *tawhid*. How might this be so? In effect it is the figure of Christ that leads, in the first instance, to the problematic of unity. So long as there is belief in one God, but also a belief in the divinity of Christ – and then, added to that, the divinity of the Holy Spirit—there is a genuine problem of accounting for divine unity to be resolved. The early affirmation of the divinity of Christ as the Son of God led to the issue of the unity of God. The Trinitarian issue emerged alongside the Christological. Although dogmatic formulations were the official outcome, and these have shaped and flavored the nature of Christianity as a belief system ever since, arguably neither unity problematic is yet fully resolved. For both Christianity and Islam unity is the foundational notion, yet the priority of divine unity remains an issue for Christian theology and, of course, is a significant issue for any Christian-Muslim theological dialogue.

## Conclusion

Does dialogue make a difference? Does relationship building produce any real beneficial effects? The skeptical reaction tends to call the dialogical enterprise into question: what is the point of it? This critique cannot go unanswered. It throws up a further challenge and contributes a particular dimension to Christian–Muslim relations, for example. In this regard Richard Bulliet has attempted to make the case for a fresh re-think of the relationship between the so-called Christian West and the world of Islam— a timely counterpoint to the standard and somewhat pessimistic appraisals of this most critical of international relations.[31] Goddard has usefully identified six dimensions of dialogical relations that obtain between Islam and Christianity—theological, philosophical, historical, social, political and cultural.[32] We have here been primarily concerned with the theological dimension. And while the term "dialogue" attracts an assumption of intellectual discursive engagement, in fact dialogue itself is multi-faceted, broadening out to many modalities and relationship types. Thus, not all modes of encounter and interaction between Christianity and Islam are "dialogical," strictly speaking, and not all dialogue is obviously theological in nature or content. Nevertheless, in today's world dialogical encounter, of all sorts and types, including especially theological, between Muslims and Christians is of vital concern to both, and this for two interrelated rea-

31. Bulliet, *Case for Islamo-Christian Civilization.*
32. Goddard, "Christian-Muslim Relations."

sons: to ameliorate trajectories of antipathy and hostility for the sake of peaceful co-existence that actually honors the deepest and best values and aspirations of these two religions; and to do that by addressing and seeking to resolve conceptually the underlying ideological, philosophical, and theological distinctions and conflicts.

Clearly there is much to be thought about and carefully considered. It would be—indeed, often is—simply easier to ignore theological issues on the grounds that there are more important ethical and practical matters to engage with dialogically. But this is to overlook the pivotal part played in the religious worldview—so the life of values and actions—of key foundational beliefs, axioms, and ideas. Theological dialogue needs to probe beyond the presented data of our traditions to the dynamics that both underlie and inhere to them. The context of religious plurality in which, today, more and more people live in consequence of demographic, socio-economic, and other changes, and the upsurge of socio-political activity involving religion, suggest more, not less, external impetus for dialogical engagement.

## Epilogue

# Religious Demography and the Future of Christian-Muslim Dialogue

## Todd M. Johnson

CHRISTIANS AND MUSLIMS TOGETHER will soon make up two thirds of the world's population. The relationship between followers of these two Abrahamic religions is impacted by a number of trends in global religious demography,[1] some of them counterintuitive. There are significant demographic trends in all religions, Christianity, and Islam that help to frame challenges in Christian-Muslim relations. While this chapter focuses on Christians and Muslims, in a literal sense the whole world is affected by how well people in these two religions interrelate.

### Trends in all Religions

*The world is becoming more religious.* In 1910, over 99 percent of the world's population was religious.[2] By 2017 this had fallen below 88 percent. But the high point for the nonreligious was around 1970, when almost 20 percent of the world's population was either agnostic or atheist. The collapse of Communism in the late-twentieth century means that the world is more religious today than in 1970.[3] Since religious people represent the vast

---

1. See Johnson and Grim, *World's Religions in Figures* for methodology in counting religionists.

2. Data for this article are found in Johnson and Grim, eds., *World Religion Database*.

3. See Toft et al., *God's Century*.

majority of the world's population it is important both to understand and to interact with people of religious traditions other than one's own. At the same time, the remaining 12 percent are agnostics and atheists[4] who also need to be treated with respect and dignity, regardless of how vitriolic a small number have been in attacking religion.

*Over the past century the fastest-growing "religion" was the nonreligious.* According to Table 1 below, world population grew at an average rate of 1.32 percent annually from 1900 to 2015. Over the same period, agnostics grew at an average annual rate of 4.83 percent and atheists 5.72 percent. More recently, however, agnostics and atheists are growing much more slowly: 0.31 percent and 0.01 percent, respectively, for the period 2000–2015, compared to world population growth averaging 1.22 percent annually. In contrast, Muslims increased by 1.95 percent per year while the Baha'i grew by 1.76 percent. Christians, adherents of the world's largest religion, increased by 1.32 percent annually over the same time period. These trends show again that the number of people who profess a religion is growing in the global context, with all religions currently gaining more adherents than they are losing.

Table 1. World religions by adherents, 1900–2015

| Religion | Adherents 1900 | % | Adherents 2015 | % | 1900–2015 % p.a. | 2000–15 % p.a. |
|---|---|---|---|---|---|---|
| Agnostics | 3,029,000 | 0.2 | 687,258,000 | 9.4 | 4.83 | 0.31 |
| Atheists | 226,000 | 0.0 | 136,084,000 | 1.9 | 5.72 | 0.01 |
| Baha'is | 205,000 | 0.0 | 7,881,000 | 0.1 | 3.23 | 1.76 |
| Buddhists | 126,956,000 | 7.8 | 515,718,000 | 7.0 | 1.23 | 0.91 |
| Chinese folk-religionists | 379,974,000 | 23.5 | 445,877,000 | 6.1 | 0.14 | 0.27 |
| Christians | 558,131,000 | 34.5 | 2,416,242,000 | 32.9 | 1.28 | 1.32 |
| Confucianists | 840,000 | 0.1 | 8,499,000 | 0.1 | 2.03 | 0.51 |
| Ethnoreligionists | 117,437,000 | 7.3 | 267,297,000 | 3.6 | 0.72 | 1.21 |
| Hindus | 202,973,000 | 12.5 | 1,007,081,000 | 13.7 | 1.40 | 1.36 |
| Jains | 1,324,000 | 0.1 | 5,984,000 | 0.1 | 1.32 | 1.49 |

4. For a technical treatment of people who self-identify with "no religion," see Zurlo and Johnson, "Unaffiliated, Yet Religious."

Table 1. World religions by adherents, 1900–2015

| | | | | | | |
|---|---|---|---|---|---|---|
| Jews | 12,292,000 | 0.8 | 14,665,000 | 0.2 | 0.15 | 0.83 |
| Muslims | 199,818,000 | 12.3 | 1,720,516,000 | 23.4 | 1.89 | 1.95 |
| New religionists | 5,986,000 | 0.4 | 65,055,000 | 0.9 | 2.10 | 0.33 |
| Shintoists | 6,720,000 | 0.4 | 2,822,000 | 0.0 | -0.75 | 0.07 |
| Sikhs | 2,962,000 | 0.2 | 25,231,000 | 0.3 | 1.88 | 1.57 |
| Spiritists | 269,000 | 0.0 | 14,474,000 | 0.2 | 3.53 | 0.95 |
| Daoists | 375,000 | 0.0 | 8,589,000 | 0.1 | 2.76 | 1.28 |
| Zoroastrians | 109,000 | 0.0 | 198,000 | 0.0 | 0.52 | 0.53 |
| Total population | 1,619,625,000 | 100.0 | 7,349,472,000 | 100.0 | 1.32 | 1.22 |

Data Source: Johnson and Grim, eds., *World Religion Database.*

*Asia is the most religiously diverse continent.* Religious diversity can be measured by different means.[5] A simple tally of how many religions in a country or region claim more than a given percentage of the total population is one helpful method. Significant diversity is found in Asia, where six countries have five or more religions with more than 5 percent of the population (Viet Nam, China, South Korea, Malaysia, Taiwan, and Brunei). The greatest religious diversity is found in Southeast Asia and Korea, where South Korea has five religions over 10 percent of the population and Viet Nam, North Korea, and Singapore each have four. At the same time, religious diversity is increasing in most countries.

*Migration is increasing religious and ethnic diversity around the world.* More than 200 million people are on the move today, carrying with them their cultural and religious backgrounds.[6] At least 860 million have now settled permanently outside of their culture's main country. Christians and Muslims, though currently 55 percent of the world's population, represent over 75 percent of all migrants.[7] Christians and Muslims, then, find

5. See Johnson and Grim, *World's Religions in Figures*, 93–110.

6. See Goldin, *Exceptional People.*

7. *Faith on the Move*, a study by the Pew Research Center's Forum on Religion & Public Life, focuses on the religious affiliation of international migrants, examining patterns of migration among seven major groups. "Migration, Religious Diasporas, and Religious Diversity" by Johnson and Zurlo (formerly Bellofatto) focuses on the 859 million settled in diaspora.

themselves as guests in new places around the world as well as hosts in countries where they have lived for centuries.

## Trends In Christianity

*Christianity has shifted dramatically to the South.* Since the early-twentieth century, Christians have made up approximately one third of the world's population. However, this masks dramatic changes in the geography of global Christianity. Table 2 shows the shift in demographics by continent from 1900 to 2015. While 68 percent of all Christians lived in Europe in 1900, by 2015 only 24 percent lived there. By contrast, less than 2 percent of all Christians lived in Africa in 1900, skyrocketing to almost 24 percent by 2015. The Global North (defined as Europe and Northern America) contained 82 percent of all Christians in 1900, falling to 35 percent by 2015.[8]

Much has been written about the impact of the shift to the South.[9] Could the shift of Christianity to the Global South open up new possibilities for the life and health of Christianity around the world? For the past century, Europeans and Americans have dominated the global Christian landscape. With this in view, Malaysian Methodist bishop Hwa Yung asked, is the future of Asian Christianity one of "bananas"—where Asian Christians are yellow on the outside but white on the inside (e.g., Chinese Christians trained by Westerners)—or one of mangoes—where Asian Christians are yellow on the outside *and* yellow on the inside (Chinese Christians with a Chinese worldview)?[10] Is the demographic shift of Christianity complete if it is not accompanied by theological reflection from fresh cultural perspectives of more recent members of global Christianity?

8. For detailed statistics, maps, and charts see Johnson and Ross, eds., *Atlas of Global Christianity*, 50–65.

9. See especially the works of Andrew Walls, Lamin Sanneh, Philip Jenkins, and Mark Noll.

10. See Yung, *Mangoes or Bananas?*

Table 2. Christians (C) by United Nations continent and Global North/South, 1900–2015

| Region | Population 1900 | C 1900 | % C 1900 | % all Xns | Population 2015 | C 2015 | % C 2015 | % all Xns |
|---|---|---|---|---|---|---|---|---|
| Global South | 1,135,392,000 | 98,674,000 | 8.7 | 18 | 6,253,192,000 | 1,564,411,000 | 25.0 | 65 |
| Africa | 107,808,000 | 9,918,000 | 9.2 | 2 | 1,186,178,000 | 574,519,000 | 48.4 | 24 |
| Asia | 956,196,000 | 21,914,000 | 2.3 | 4 | 4,393,296,000 | 376,015,000 | 8.6 | 16 |
| Latin America | 65,142,000 | 62,003,000 | 95.2 | 11 | 634,387,000 | 585,490,000 | 92.3 | 24 |
| Oceania | 6,246,000 | 4,839,000 | 77.5 | 1 | 39,331,000 | 28,387,000 | 72.2 | 1 |
| Global North | 484,233,000 | 459,457,000 | 94.9 | 82 | 1,096,280,000 | 851,831,000 | 77.7 | 35 |
| North America | 81,626,000 | 78,812,000 | 96.6 | 14 | 357,838,000 | 275,095,000 | 76.9 | 11 |
| Europe | 402,607,000 | 380,645,000 | 94.5 | 68 | 738,442,000 | 576,736,000 | 78.1 | 24 |
| Globe | 1,619,625,000 | 558,131,000 | 34.5 | 100 | 7,349,472,000 | 2,416,242,000 | 32.9 | 100 |

Data Source: Johnson and Grim, eds., *World Religion Database.*

*Christianity is fragmented.* Christians are now found in nearly 45,000 denominations. These range in size from millions of members to fewer than one hundred members.[11] Note that the vast majority of denominations are in the Independent and Protestant traditions. By 2025, there will likely be 55,000 denominations. A major challenge for Christians is how they deal with this diversity—by unhealthy competition or useful collaboration.

*Christians speak a multitude of languages.* Spanish is the number-one mother tongue of Christianity and has been for several decades. The others in the top five are English, Portuguese, Russian, and Mandarin. Note that many non-Western languages are climbing up the list of the top twenty-five mother tongues such as Tagalog, Amharic, Korean, and Yoruba.[12] While Bible translation has been a major focus of linguists, there are implications for theology, ecclesiology, and hymnody.[13]

*Christians in the Middle East are declining.* Christians represented 13.6 percent of the Middle East's population in 1910 but only 4.2 percent in 2010. By 2025, they will likely constitute less than 3.6 percent of the region.[14] Their diminishing presence is troubling when viewed in light of centuries of relative demographic stability: from 1500 to 1900, Christians were approximately 15 percent of the region's population. In addition, the Middle East is the historic geographical origin of Christianity (as well as two other Abrahamic faiths: Judaism and Islam).

## Trends in Islam

*Muslims have increased by eight times in 115 years and almost doubled as a percentage of the world's population.* In 1900 there were 200 million Muslims in the world. By 2015 this had grown to 1.7 billion. This represents a growth from 12.3 percent of the world's population in 1900 to 23.4 percent by 2015. Over the century, world population has grown by 1.38 percent p.a. whereas Muslims have grown at 1.89 percent p.a. Studies have shown that the majority of this growth has been the result of high birth rates.[15]

11. These are listed for each of the world's 234 countries in Johnson and Zurlo, *World Christian Database.*

12. A list of top mother tongues can be found in Johnson and Ross, eds., *Atlas of Global Christianity*, 213.

13. See Jenkins, *New Faces of Christianity.*

14. See Johnson and Zurlo, "Ongoing Exodus."

15. See Lipka and Hackett, "Why Muslims."

*Most Muslims live in Asia, but they are growing around the world.* The fastest growth of Muslims is found in Oceania (which includes Australia), but the numbers are still small. Africa has the next-fastest rate. From 1910–2010, Africa's share of the world's Muslims increased from 18 percent to 27 percent. Nonetheless, Indonesia is the country with the most Muslims, followed by India, Pakistan, and Bangladesh. The six countries with the most Muslims are all in Asia. The next 4 are in Africa.

*Muslims speak languages other than Arabic.* The top five mother tongues of Islam are Bengali, Urdu, Western Panjabi, Turkish, and Javanese, representing over a quarter of all Muslims worldwide.[16] One of the many forms of Arabic (Egyptian) appears only at number six. While Arabic remains central to the Muslim faith, other languages are important in the everyday lives of Muslims around the world.

*Europe is not becoming Muslim, but the Muslim minority is influential.* Only 6 percent of Europe's population is Muslim and this is expected to rise to just 8 percent by 2030. But the Muslim minority has a disproportionate impact in politics and society. In some countries, Islam is expected to grow significantly over the next twenty years (e.g., Macedonia, Sweden, and Belgium).[17]

*The number of Muslims in the United States is disputed.* The Pew Research Center estimates that there were 3.3 million Muslims in the United States in 2015.[18] Other estimates run as high as seven million.[19] The World Religion Database estimates 4.4 million, which includes Muslim immigrants from around the world, African-Americans who have converted to Islam, and formerly non-Muslim women married to Muslim men. The United States, a majority Christian country with religious freedom, offers an excellent venue for Christian-Muslim relations.

## Trends in Christian-Muslim Interactions

*Christians and Muslims together have increased from only a third of the world's population and could soon be two thirds.* In 1800, Christians and Muslims together represented only 33 percent of the world's population. Estimates for 2017 show that Christians and Muslims together now represent 57

16. See Johnson and Ross, eds., *Atlas of Global Christianity*, 215.

17. See Hackett et al., *Changing Global Religious Landscape.*

18. See Mohamed, "New Estimate."

19. For example, Bagby, *American Mosque 2011*, 4.

percent of the world's population. By 2050, the figure could be as high as 64 percent. Note that in 2050, Christians (35 percent) will likely still be larger than Muslims (29 percent).[20] While Muslims continue to have higher birth rates, conversions to Christianity are expected to be significant, especially in China and India. China's Christians are poised to increase from today's 120 million (9 percent of the population) to about 220 million by 2050 (16 percent). In India, the current total of 62 million (4.7 percent) is set to grow to 110 million (6.5 percent) by 2050. For Muslims, the largest populations will continue to be found in Asia (India, Pakistan, Indonesia, Bangladesh).

*Muslims do not often feel at home in majority Christian countries.* As stated earlier, migration has taken Muslims from their traditional homes in Africa and Asia and thrust them into the Western World: Europe, North America, and Australia/New Zealand. While some have welcomed them, many Westerners hold strong anti-immigrant ideas.[21] In recent years, these appear to have strengthened, making it hard for Muslim immigrants to integrate.

*Christians are persecuted, sometimes in majority Muslim countries.*

Christians who have been living as minorities in both African and Asian countries have been experiencing increasing persecution. Many of these countries are predominantly Muslim. Studies have shown that persecution has increased in recent years, with many Christians forced to leave their homelands.[22]

*Christians and Muslims do not know each other.* Recent research reveals that as many as 86 percent of all Muslims, Hindus, and Buddhists do

---

20. The Pew Research Center released a report on April 2, 2015 on *The Future of World Religions*, consisting of population projections between 2010 and 2050. A major finding of the report is that by 2050 Christian and Muslim populations will be nearly the same size—2.9 billion and 2.7 billion, respectively—with no change in the percentage of the world that is Christian (31.4 percent). There are several reasons for the discrepancy between Pew's and the World Religion Database's estimates of Christians in 2050. The WRD taps into knowledge from contacts in every country of the world who inform us on what is happening in non-traditional forms of Christianity, such as house churches and insider movements (where individuals convert to Christianity in secret and/or remain identified with their past religion). Some of the most significant growth of Christianity in the world today, and into the future, is indeed non-traditional and does not easily get picked up in traditional demographic measures such as censuses, surveys, and polls. This is particularly the case in China and India.

21. See, for example, Kunzig, "New Europeans."

22. See Brown, "Minority Report."

not personally know a Christian.[23] Other research shows a gap in friendship and hospitality between Christians and Muslims, where closest friends are found among co-religionists.[24] While this is not surprising, it is at the personal level where Christians and Muslims will discover common interests and build solidarity.

## Improving Christian-Muslim Relations

*Rethink Christian and Muslim identity.* We have many dimensions in our identities. Our citizenship, residence, geographic origin, gender, class, politics, profession, employment, food habits, sports interests, taste in music, social commitments, and a host of other factors make us members of a variety of groups simultaneously. At the same time, as we see that some people identify as members of one religion and others of another, we have to be cautious about how this identity is understood. Amartya Sen laments that the world is increasingly seen as a federation of religions or civilizations, ignoring all the other ways in which people see themselves. He writes, "Underlying this line of thinking is the odd presumption that the people of the world can be uniquely categorized according to some singular and overarching system of portioning . . . [this] solitarist approach can be a good way of misunderstanding nearly everyone in the world."[25] It is important for us to see that religion is often used to divide people when they might have commonalities in other aspects of their identities. Christians and Muslims have more in common than is usually assumed.

*Empower Christians and Muslims to interact in religiously diverse communities.* Christians and Muslims will improve their engagement with others through developing a "theology of interfaith solidarity." A theology of interfaith solidarity does not have to concede that all religions lead up the same proverbial mountain trail(s) to God or deny that real conflict will arise. Rather, it is a starting point to focus on building bridges between people of different faiths instead of debating which bridge leads to heaven.[26] It begins with shared values, developing trust first, and then working toward deeper conversations and common concerns. Eboo Patel, Founder

23. See "Personal Contact" in Johnson and Ross, eds., *Atlas of Global Christianity*, 316–19.

24. See Pew Research Center, *World's Muslims*.

25. Sen, *Identity and Violence*, xii, 5.

26. Patel, *Sacred Ground*, 79.

and President of Interfaith Youth Core, a service organization for college students, is a leading voice in American interfaith relations. He maintains that every individual must be welcome to express his or her faith honestly and candidly.

*Deepen knowledge on world religions.* Christians and Muslims know very little about each other's religions. According to the 2010 Pew Forum U.S. Religious Knowledge Survey, atheists and agnostics have more religious knowledge than religious followers.[27] We would do well in both communities to better understand the religions of the world.[28] Of particular importance for Christians and Muslims is their mutual understanding of who God is, how they relate to him, and how they relate to each other.

*Practice hospitality and civility.* Too much attention is given to conflict between Muslims and the West (or Christians). While good relations between the Western World and the Muslim World are important, Christians and Muslims should know and love their neighbors. Christians and Muslims also have a chance to learn to treat each other better. Hospitality, reduced to entertaining friends of the same social strata, has lost much of its sacramental and covenantal quality, becoming rather ordinary. Theologian and ethicist Christine Pohl defines ordinary hospitality as the act of inviting friends over to solidify relationships, reinforce social boundaries, and anticipate repayment. By contrast, hospitality across social boundaries reflects divine generosity, anticipating the hospitality of God. This type of covenantal hospitality is socially transformative. Pohl writes,

> The most transformative expressions of hospitality, both historically and in our time, are associated with hosts who are liminal, marginal, or at the lower end of the social order. These hosts are essentially threshold or bridge people, connected in some ways to the larger society but distinct from it . . . . Without these crucial dimensions of marginality or liminality, hospitality serves its normal function in reinforcing social boundaries."[29]

Christians and Muslims can draw on theological justifications both to host each other in their homes and to form significant friendships.

---

27. Pew Research Center, "Who Knows What."
28. See Prothero, *God Is Not One.*
29. Pohl, *Making Room,* 105–6.

## Conclusion

In the twentieth century many sociologists predicted the demise of religion. Not only has religion survived, it has thrived. The result is a world that is religiously diverse and complex. In order for Christians and Muslims to navigate the crossroads of a multi-faith world, we must understand how to view ourselves and others religiously. Many Christians want to engage the world but are concerned about how to maintain a strong Christian identity. The same is true for Muslims. In a globalized world, Christians and Muslims must work together with others to address globalized problems. We should look for ways in which Christians and Muslims might be more expansive in their relationships with others—approaches based not in hostility but in benevolence. The future of the world depends on it.

# Bibliography

'Abd al-Jabbar. *Critique of Christian Origins*. Translated by Gabriel Said Reynolds and Samir Khalil Samir. Islamic Translation Series. Provo, UT: Brigham Young University Press, 2010.

Abu Qurra, Theodore. *Mujadala Abi Qurra ma'a al-mutakallimin al-muslimin fi Majlis al-khalifa al-ma'mun (Dispute of Theodore Abu Qurra with the Muslim Theologians in the Salon of the Caliph al-Ma'mun)*. Edited by Ignace Dick. Aleppo, 2007.

Accad, Fouad Elias. *Building Bridges: Christianity and Islam*. Colorado Springs: NavPress, 1997.

Accad, Martin. "Corruption and/or Misinterpretation of the Bible: The Story of the Islamic Usage of Tahrif." *Theological Review—Beirut* (2003) 67–96.

Afsaruddin, Asma. *The First Muslims: History and Memory*. Oxford: Oneworld, 2008.

———. "The Hermeneutics of Inter-Faith Relations: Retrieving Moderation and Pluralism as Universal Principles in Qur'anic Exegeses." *Journal of Religious Ethics* 37/2 (2009) 331–54.

———. "The 'Upright Community': Interpreting the Righteousness and Salvation of the People of the Book in the Qur'an." In *Jewish-Muslim Relations in Past and Present: A Kaleidoscopic View*, edited by Josef Meri, 48–71. Leiden: Brill, 2017.

Ahmed, Shahab. *What Is Islam? The Importance of Being Islamic*. Princeton, NJ: Princeton University Press, 2016.

Akbarzadeh, Shahram, and Samina Yasmeen, editors. *Islam and the West: Reflections from Australia*. Sydney: UNSW, 2005.

Algar, Hamid. *Wahhabism: A Critical Essay*. New York: Islamic Publications International, 2002.

Alhabshi, Othman, and Nik Mustapha Nik Hassan. *Islam and Tolerance*. Kuala Lumpur: Institute of Islamic Understanding Malaysia, 1994.

Ali, Merad. "Le Christ selon le Coran." *Revue de l'Occident Musulman et de la Méditerranée* 5 (1968) 79–94.

al-Anbari, Abu al-Barakat Abd al-Rahman ibn Muhammad. *Nuzhat al-'adibba' fi tabaqat al-'udaba'*. Edited by Attia Amer. Stockholm: Almqwist and Wiksell, 1963.

Anderson, Benedict. *Imagined Communities: Reflections on the Origin and Spread of Nationalism*. London: Verso, 1983.

Anthony, Sean W. "Muhammad, Menahem, and the Paraclete: New Light on Ibn Ishaq's (d. 150/767) Arabic version of John 15:23—16:1." *Bulletin of SOAS* 79/2 (2016) 255–78.

Aquinas, Thomas. *Summa theologiae*. Vol. 2, *Existence and Nature of God (1a2–11)*. Edited and translated by Timothy McDermott. London: Blackfriars, 1963.

Arnaldez, Roger. *A la croisée des trois monothéismes: une communauté de pensée au Moyen Age.* Paris: Albin Michel, 1993.

Augustine. *De civitate Dei.* Patrologiae latina 41. Edited by J.-P. Migne. Paris: 1864.

Ayoub, Mahmoud. "Christian-Muslim Dialogue." In *A Muslim View of Christianity: Essays on Dialogue by Mahmoud Ayoub,* edited by Irfan A. Omar, 64–69. New York: Orbis, 2007.

———. "The Idea of Redemption in Christianity and Islam." In *A Muslim View of Christianity: Essays on Dialogue by Mahmoud Ayoub,* edited by Irfan A. Omar, 90–97. New York: Orbis, 2007.

———. "Jesus the Son of God: A Study of the Terms *Ibn* and *Walad* in the Qur'an and *Tafsir* Tradition." In *A Muslim View of Christianity: Essays on Dialogue by Mahmoud Ayoub,* edited by Irfan A. Omar, 117–33. New York: Orbis, 2007.

———. "The Need for Harmony and Collaboration between Muslims and Christians." In *A Muslim View of Christianity: Essays on Dialogue by Mahmoud Ayoub,* edited by Irfan A. Omar, 9–16. New York: Orbis, 2007.

———. "Roots of Muslim-Christian Conflict." In *A Muslim View of Christianity: Essays on Dialogue by Mahmoud Ayoub,* edited by Irfan A. Omar, 42–63. New York: Orbis, 2007.

———. "Toward an Islamic Christology II." In *A Muslim View of Christianity: Essays on Dialogue by Mahmoud Ayoub,* edited by Irfan A. Omar, 156–83. New York: Orbis, 2007.

Azaiez, Mehdi. *Le contre-discours coranique.* Berlin: De Gruyter, 2015.

Azumah, John. "The Divine and Human Origins of the Bible." In *Communicating the Word: Revelation, Translation, and Interpretation in Christianity and Islam,* edited by David Marshall, 92–97. Washington, DC: Georgetown University Press, 2011.

Bagby, Ihsan. *The American Mosque 2011: Basic Characteristics of the American Mosque, Attitudes of Mosque Leaders.* Report 1 from the US Mosque Survey 2011. Washington, DC: Council on American Islamic Relations, 2012. https://www.cair.com/images/pdf/The-American-Mosque-2011-part-1.pdf.

Basetti Sani, Giulio. *Il Corano Nella Luce di Cristo: Saggio per una Reinterpretazione Cristiana del Libro Sacro dell'Islam.* Bologna: EMI, 1972.

Bauschke, Martin. "A Christian View of Islam." In *Islam and Inter-Faith Relations,* edited by Perry Schmidt-Leukel and Lloyd Ridgeon, 137–55. London: SCM, 2007.

Beaumont, Mark. "Christian Views of Muhammad since the Publication of Kenneth Cragg's *Muhammad and the Christian, A Question of Response* in 1984." *Transformation* 32 (2015) 145–62.

Bennett, Clinton. *Studying Islam: The Critical Issues.* London: Continuum, 2010.

———. *Understanding Christian-Muslim Relations: Past and Present.* London: Continuum, 2008.

Blachère, Regis. *Dans les pas de Mahomet.* Paris: Hachette, 1956.

Block, Corrie. *The Qur'an in Christian-Muslim Dialogue: Historical and Modern Interpretations.* Oxon: Routledge, 2014.

Bottini, Laura. "The Apology of al-Kindi." In *Christian-Muslim Relations: A Bibliographical History, Volume 1 (600–900),* edited by David Thomas and Barbara Roggema, 587–94. Leiden: Brill, 2009.

Böwering, Gerhard. "Recent Research on the Construction of the Qur'an." In *The Qur'an in Its Historical Context,* edited by Gabriel Said Reynolds, 70–87. Abingdon: Routledge, 2007.

Brague, Rémi. "The Concept of the Abrahamic Religions, Problems and Pitfalls." In *The Oxford Handbook of the Abrahamic Religions*, edited by Adam J. Silverstein and Guy G. Stroumsa, 88–105. Oxford: Oxford University Press, 2015.

———. *Du Dieu des chrétiens de d'un ou deux autres*. Paris: Flammarion, 2008.

Bridger, J. Scott. *Christian Exegesis of the Qur'an: A Critical Analysis of the Apologetic Use of the Qur'an in Select Medieval and Contemporary Arabic Texts*. Cambridge: James Clarke, 2016.

Brown, Elijah M. "Minority Report: Christian Persecution in Muslim-Majority Countries." Fuller Studio, 2017. https://fullerstudio.fuller.edu/minority-report-christian-persecution-muslim-majoirty-countries/.

Bulliet, Richard W. *The Case for Islamo-Christian Civilization*. New York: Columbia University Press, 2004.

Bulus al-Rahib al-Antaki. "Letter to a Muslim Friend." In *Muslim-Christian Polemic during the Crusades: The Letter from the People of Cyprus and Ibn Abi Talib al-Dimashqi's Response*, edited by Rifaat Ebied and David Thomas, 54–147. Leiden: Brill, 2005.

Burrell, David B. *Aquinas: God and Action*. Notre Dame, IN: University of Notre Dame Press, 1979.

———. *Knowing the Unknowable God: Ibn-Sina, Maimonides, Aquinas*. Notre Dame, IN: University of Notre Dame Press, 1986.

Carroll, John T. *Jesus and the Gospels: An Introduction*. Louisville: Westminster/John Knox, 2016.

Caspar, Robert. *A Historical Introduction to Islamic Theology*. Rome: Pontificio Istituto di Studi Arabi ed'Islamistica, 2002.

*Catechism of the Catholic Church*. Nairobi: Paulines, 1992.

Chadwick, Henry. *The Early Church*. London: Penguin, 1967.

Cragg, Kenneth. *Jesus and the Muslim: An Exploration*. Oxford: Oneworld, 1999.

———. *The Mind of the Qur'an: Chapters in Reflection*. London: Allen and Unwin, 1973.

———. *Muhammad and the Christian: A Question of Response*. London: Darton, Longman and Todd, 1984.

———. *The Weight in the Word: Prophethood: Biblical and Quranic*. Brighton: Sussex Academic, 1999.

Cranfield, Charles E. B. *Romans: A Shorter Commentary*. Edinburgh: T. & T. Clark, 1985.

Crossan, John Dominic. *The Greatest Prayer: Rediscovering the Revolutionary Message of the Lord's Prayer*. New York: HarperCollins, 2010.

Cutsinger, James S. "Disagreeing to Agree: A Christian Response to 'A Common Word.'" In *Muslim and Christian Understanding: Theory and Application of "A Common Word,"* edited by Waleed El-Ansary and David K. Linnan, 111–30. New York: Palgrave Macmillan, 2010.

Davids, Adelbert, and Pim Valkenberg. "John of Damascus: The Heresy of the Ishmaelites." In *The Routledge Reader in Christian-Muslim Relations*, edited by Mona Siddiqui, 8–32. London: Routledge, 2013.

Davies, Noel, and Martin Conway, editors. *World Christianity in the Twentieth Century: A Reader*. London: SCM, 2008.

Day, John. "Hosea and the Baal Cult." In *Prophecy and the Prophets in Ancient Israel*, edited by John Day, 202–24. London: T. & T. Clark, 2010.

D'Costa, Gavin. "The Nature and Purpose of the Christian Community (the Church)." In *The Community of Believers*, edited by Lucinda Mosher and David Marshall, 3–14. Washington, DC: Georgetown University Press, 2015.

————. *Vatican II: Catholic Doctrines on Jews and Muslims.* Oxford: Oxford University Press, 2014.

Denny, F. M. "*Ummah* in the Constitution of Medina." *Journal of Near Eastern Studies* 36/1 (1977) 39–47.

de Blois, Francis. "Book Review: Die Syro-Aramäische Lesart des Koran. Ein Beitrag zur Entschlüsselung der Koransprache." *Journal of Qur'anic Studies* 5/1 (2003) 92–97.

di Matteo, I. "Il 'tahrif' od alterazione della Bibbia secondo i musulmani." *Bessarione* 38 (1922) 64–111, 223–60.

Donner, Fred. *Muhammad and the Believers.* Cambridge, MA: Belknap, 2010.

Dulles, Avery. *Models of the Church: A Critical Assessment of the Church in All Its Aspects.* New York: Doubleday, 1974.

Dunlop, D. M. "A Christian Mission to Muslim Spain in the XVIth Century." *Al-Andalus* 17 (1952) 259–310.

Dupuis, Jacque. *Toward a Christian Theology of Religious Pluralism.* Maryknoll, NY: Orbis, 1997.

Ebied, Rifaat, and David Thomas, editors. *Muslim-Christian Polemic during the Crusades: The Letter from the People of Cyprus and Ibn Abi Talib al-Dimashqi's Response.* Leiden: Brill, 2005.

Ehrman, Bart. *Lost Christianities: The Battles for Scriptures and the Faiths We Never Knew.* New York: Oxford University Press, 2003.

Eiedat, Moh'd Khair. "The Amman Message: A Counter-Narrative to Islamic Fundamentalism." In *Muslim Identity in a Turbulent Age*, edited by Mike Hardy et al., 151–59. London: Jessica Kingsley, 2017.

Elias, Jamal J. *Islam.* London: Routledge, 2005.

Esack, Farid. *Qur'an, Liberation & Pluralism: An Islamic Perspective of Interreligious Solidarity against Oppression.* Oxford: Oneworld, 1997.

Farhadian, Charles E., editor. *Introducing World Christianity.* Oxford: Wiley-Blackwell, 2012.

al-Faruqi, Isma'il. *Islam and Other Faiths.* Leicester: Islamic Foundation, 1998.

————. "On the Nature of Islamic Da'wah." In *Christian Mission and Islamic Da'wah: Proceedings of the Chambésy Dialogue Consultation*, 33–51. Leicester: Islamic Foundation, 1982.

Fee, Gordon D. *The First Epistle to the Corinthians.* Rev. ed. Grand Rapids: Eerdmans, 2014.

Firestone, Reuven. *Who Are the Real Chosen People?: The Meaning of Chosenness in Judaism, Christianity, and Islam.* Woodstock, VT: Skylight Paths, 2008.

Galindo Aguilar, Emilio. "The Second International Muslim-Christian Congress of Cordoba (March 21–27, 1977)." In *Christianity and Islam: The Struggling Dialogue*, edited by Richard W. Rousseau, 161–83. Scranton, PA: Ridge Row, 1985.

Gardner, Lucy. "Perspectives on Christian Desires for Communion and Experiences of Division (or, The History of the Church in Half a Chapter!)." In *The Community of Believers*, edited by Lucinda Mosher and David Marshall, 45–64. Washington, DC: Georgetown University Press, 2015.

Gaudeul, Jean-Marie. "The Correspondence between Leo and Umar: Umar's Letter Re-Discovered?" *Islamochristiana* 10 (1984) 109–57.

————. *Encounters and Clashes: Islam and Christianity in History.* Rome: Pontificio Istituto di Studi Arabi e d'Islamistica, 2000.

————. *Riposte aux Chretiens*. Rome: Pontificio Istituto di Studi Arabi e d'Islamistica, 1995.

Gaudeul, Jean-Marie, and Robert Caspar. "Textes de la tradition musulmane concernant le tahrif (falsification) des ecritures." *Islamochristiana* 6 (1980) 61–104.

Ghattas, Raouf G., and Carol Ghattas. *A Christian Guide to the Qur'an: Building Bridges in Muslim Evangelism*. Grand Rapids: Kregel, 2009.

Goddard, Hugh. *Christians and Muslims: From Double Standards to Mutual Understanding*. Surrey: Curzon, 1995.

————. "Christian-Muslim Relations: Yesterday, Today, and Tomorrow." *International Journal for the Study of the Christian Church* 3/2 (2003) 1–14.

————. *A History of Christian-Muslim Relations*. Chicago: New Amsterdam, 2000.

Goldin, Ian. *Exceptional People: How Migration Shaped Our World and Will Define the Future*. Princeton, NJ: Princeton University Press, 2011.

Goshen-Gottstein, Alon. "God between Christians and Jews: Is It the Same God?" In *Do We Worship the Same God? Jews, Christians, and Muslims in Dialogue*, edited by Miroslav Volf, 50–75. Grand Rapids: Eerdmans, 2012.

Griffith, Sidney. *The Church in the Shadow of the Mosque: Christians and Muslims in the World of Islam*. Princeton, NJ: Princeton University Press, 2008.

————. "Syriacisms in the 'Arabic Qur'an': Who Were 'Those Who Said "Allah Is Third of Three"' according to Al-Ma'ida 73?" In *A Word Fitly Spoken: Studies in Mediaeval Exegesis of the Hebrew Bible and the Qur'an*, edited by Meir M. Bar-Asher, Simon Hopkins, Sarah Stroumsa, and Bruno Chiesa, 83–110. Jerusalem: Ben-Zvi Institute, 2007.

Guezzou, Mokrane. *Al-Wahidi's Asbab al-Nuzul*. Louisville: Fons Vitae, 2008.

Guthrie, Shirley C. *Christian Doctrine*. Rev. ed. Louisville: Westminster/John Knox, 1994.

Güzelmansur, Timo, editor. *Das koranische Motiv der Schriftfälschung (tahrif) durch Juden und Christen: Islamische Deutungen und christliche Reaktionen*. Regensburg: Friedrich Pustet, 2014.

Gyekye, Kwame. *African Cultural Values: An Introduction*. Accra-Ghana: Sankofa, 1996.

Hackett, Conrad, et al. *The Changing Global Religious Landscape*. Pew Research Center, April 5, 2017. http://www.pewforum.org/2017/04/05/the-changing-global-religious-landscape/.

Hahneman, Geoffrey Mark. "The Muratorian Fragment and the Origins of the New Testament Canon." In *The Canon Debate*, edited by L. McDonald and J. A. Sanders, 405–15. Peabody, MA: Hendrickson, 2002.

Hamza, Feras. "Unity and Disunity in the Life of the Muslim Community." In *The Community of Believers*, edited by Lucinda Mosher and David Marshall, 65–78. Washington, DC: Georgetown University Press, 2015.

Hardy, Mike, Fiyaz Mughal, and Sarah Markiewicz, editors. *Muslim Identity in a Turbulent Age: Islamic Extremism and Western Islamophobia*. London: Jessica Kingsley, 2017.

Hassan, Riaz. "Globalisation's Challenge to the Islamic *Ummah*." *Asian Journal of Social Science* 34/2 (2006) 311–23.

Hastings, Adrian, editor. *A World History of Christianity*. Grand Rapids: Eerdmans, 1999.

Heft, James L., Reuven Firestone, and Omid Safi, editors. *Learned Ignorance: Intellectual Humility among Jews, Christians, and Muslims*. Oxford: Oxford University Press, 2011.

Heimgartner, Martin, editor. *Timotheos I, Ostsyrischer Patriarch: Disputation mit dem Kalifen al-Mahdi: Textedition*. CSCO 631, Syr 244. Leuven: Peeters, 2011.

————. *Einleitung, Übersetzung, und Anmerkungen*. CSCO 632, Syr 245. Leuven: Peeters, 2011.

Hettema, T. L., and A. van der Kooij, editors. *Religious Polemic in Context*. Assen: Royal van Gorcum, 2004.

Hewer, C. T. R. *Understanding Islam: The First Ten Steps*. London: SCM, 2006.

Hoyland, Robert. "The Correspondence of Leo III (717–741) and 'Umar II (717–720)." *Aram* 6 (1994) 165–77.

————. "St. Andrews Ms. 14 and the Earliest Arabic *Summa Theologiae*." In *Syriac Polemics: Studies in Honour of Gerrit Jan Reinink*, edited by Wout Jac. Van Bekkum, et al., 159–72. Leuven: Peeters, 2007.

Hughes. Aaron W. *Abrahamic Religions: On the Uses and Abuses of History*. Oxford: Oxford University Press, 2012.

Hussain, Amir. "Muslims, Pluralism, and Interfaith Dialogue." In *Progressive Muslims: On Justice, Gender, and Pluralism*, edited by Omid Safi, 251–69. Oxford: Oneworld, 2003.

Hwa, Yung. *Mangoes or Bananas? The Quest for an Authentic Asian Christian Theology*. Eugene, OR: Wifpf & Stock, 1997.

Ibn Ishaq. *The Life of Muhammad: A Translation of Ishaq's Sirat Rasul Allah*. Translated by Alfred Guillaume. Oxford: Oxford University Press, 1955.

Ireland, Randall. *Inviting Muslims to Christ: A Clear Path to Salvation*. Middle East Religious Studies Foundation, 2016.

Jeffery, Arthur. "Ghevond's Text of the Correspondence between 'Umar II and Leo III." *Harvard Theological Review* 37/4 (October 1944) 269–332.

Jenkins, Philip. *The New Faces of Christianity: Believing the Bible in the Global South*. Oxford: Oxford University Press, 2006.

John Paul II, Pope. *Redemptoris missio* ["The Mission of the Redeemer"]: *On the Permanent Validity of the Church's Missionary Mandate*. Papal encyclical, December 7, 1990. http://w2.vatican.va/content/john-paul-ii/en/encyclicals/documents/hf_jp-ii_enc_07121990_redemptoris-missio.html.

————. *The Theology of the Body: Human Love in the Divine Plan*. Boston: Pauline, 1997.

Johnson, Todd M., and Brian J. Grim, editors. *World Religion Database*. Boston: Brill, August 2017. http://www.worldreligiondatabase.org.

————. *The World's Religions in Figures: An Introduction to International Religious Demography*. West Sussex: Wiley-Blackwell, 2013.

Johnson, Todd M., and Kenneth R. Ross, editors. *Atlas of Global Christianity*. Edinburgh: Edinburgh University Press, 2009.

Johnson, Todd M., and Gina A. Zurlo (formerly Bellofatto). "Migration, Religious Diasporas, and Religious Diversity: A Global Survey." *Mission Studies* 29/1 (July 2012) 3–32.

————. "Ongoing Exodus: Tracking the Emigration of Christians from the Middle East." *Harvard Journal of Middle Eastern Politics and Policy* 3 (2013–2014) 39–49.

————, editors. *World Christian Database*. Boston: Brill, 2017. http://www.worldchristiandatabase.org.

Karamustafa, Ahmet. "Islam: A Civilizational Project in Progress." In *Progressive Muslims: On Justice, Gender and Pluralism*, edited by Omid Safi, 98–110. Oxford: Oneworld, 2003.

Kärkkäinen, Veli-Matti. *Christology: A Global Introduction*. Grand Rapids: Baker Academic, 2003.

Kateregga, Badru D., and David Shenk. *A Muslim and a Christian in Dialogue: Islam and Christianity.* Nairobi: Uzima, 1980.

Keating, Sandra Toenies. "Revisiting the Charge of Tahrif: The Question of Supersessionism in Early Islam and the Qur'an." In *Nicholas of Cusa and Islam: Polemic and Dialogue in the Late Middle Ages,* edited by I. C. Levy, R. George-Tvrtkovic, and D. Duclow, 202–17. Leiden: Brill, 2014.

Khatab, Seyyed, and Gary D. Bouma. *Democracy in Islam.* London: Routledge, 2007.

Kim, Seonyoung. "The Arabic Letters of the Byzantine Emperor Leo III to the Caliph 'Umar Ibn 'Abd al-'Aziz: An Edition, Translation and Commentary." PhD diss., Catholic University of America, 2017.

Kimball, Charles. *Striving Together: A Way Forward in Christian-Muslim Relations.* New York: Orbis, 1991.

al-Kindi, 'Abd al-Masih. *Risalat 'Abdallah ibn Isma'il al-Hashimi ila 'Abd al-Masih ibn Ishaq al-Kindi yad'uhu biha ila l-Islam wa-risalat 'Abd al-Masih ila l-Hashimi yaruddubiha 'alayhi wa-yad'uhu ila l-Nasraniyya.* Edited by Anton Tien. Turkish Mission Aid Society, 1885.

Kinoshita, Sharon, and Siobhain Bly Calkin. "Saracens as Idolaters in European Vernacular Literatures." In *Christian-Muslim Relations: A Bibliographical History, Volume 4 (1200–1350),* edited by David Thomas and Alex Mallett, 29–44. Leiden: Brill, 2012.

Krokus, Christian S. *The Theology of Louis Massignon: Islam, Christ, and the Church.* Washington, DC: Catholic University of America Press, 2017.

Kunzig, Robert. "The New Europeans: Voices from a Changing Continent." *National Geographic,* October 2016. http://nationalgeographic.com/magazine/2016/10/europe-immigration-muslim-refugees-portraits/.

Kuracan, Ahmet, and Mustafa Kasum Erol. *Dialogue in Islam: Qur'an – Sunnah – History.* London: Dialogue Society, 2011.

Lambert, Jean. *Le Dieu distribué: une anthropologie compare des monothéismes.* Paris: les Éditions du Cerf, 1995.

Lausanne Movement. "Christian Witness to Muslims." Lausanne Occasional Paper 13. http://www.lausanne.org/content/lop/lop-13.

Lawrence, Bruce B. *Who Is Allah?* Chapel Hill: University of North Carolina Press, 2015.

Lazarus-Yafeh, Hava. *Intertwined Worlds: Medieval Islam and Bible Criticism.* Princeton, NJ: Princeton University Press, 1992.

———. "Tahrif." In *Encyclopedia of Islam,* edited by P. J. Bearman, Th. Bianquis, C. E. Bosworth, E. van Donzel, and W. P. Heinrichs, 10:111–12. 2nd ed. Leiden: Brill, 2000.

Leirvik, Oddbjørn. *Interreligious Studies: A Relational Approach to Religious Activism and the Study of Religions.* London: Bloomsbury, 2014.

Lipka, Michal, and Conrad Hacket. "Why Muslims Are the World's Fastest Growing Religious Group." Pew Research Center, April 6, 2017. http://www.pewresearch.org/fact-tank/2017/04/06/why-muslims-are-the-worlds-fastest-growing-religious-group/.

Long, D. Stephen. *The Perfectly Simple Triune God: Aquinas and His Legacy.* Minneapolis: Fortress, 2016.

Luxenberg, Christoph. *The Syro-Aramaic Reading of the Koran: A Contribution to the Decoding of the Language of the Koran.* Berlin: Hans Schiler, 2015.

Macquarrie, John. *Principles of Christian Theology.* 2nd ed. New York: Schribner's, 1966.

Madigan, Daniel A. "Particularity, Universality, and Finality: Insights from the Gospel of John." In *Communicating the Word: Revelation, Translation, and Interpretation in Christianity and Islam*, edited by David Marshall, 14–25. Washington, DC: Georgetown University Press, 2011.

Marmion, Declan, and Rik Van Nieuwenhove. *An Introduction to the Trinity*. Cambridge: Cambridge University Press, 2011.

Marranci, Gabrielle. *The Anthropology of Islam*. New York: Berg, 2008.

Marshall, David, editor. *Communicating the Word: Revelation, Translation, and Interpretation in Christianity and Islam*. Washington, DC: Georgetown University Press, 2011.

Marshall, I. Howard. *New Testament Theology*. Downers Grove, IL: InterVarsity, 2004.

Mawdudi, Sayyid Abul A'la. *Towards Understanding the Qur'an*. Vol. 1: *Suras 1–3*. Translated by Zafar Ishaq Ansari. Leicester: Islamic Foundation, 1988.

McAnnally-Linz, Ryan, and Mirslav Volf. "God and Allah: What's in a Name?" *Current Dialogue* 56 (December 2014) 4–8.

McAuliffe, Jane D. *The Genesis of Doctrine*. Grand Rapids: Eerdmans, 1990.

———. *Qur'anic Christians: An Analysis of Classical and Modern Exegesis*. New York: Cambridge University Press, 1991.

McCloud, Aminah Beverly. *African American Islam*. New York: Routledge, 1995.

McGrath, Alister E. *An Introduction to Christianity*. Malden, MA: Blackwell, 1997.

McKane, William, editor. *Al-Ghazali's Book of Fear and Hope*. Leiden: Brill, 1965.

McKim, D. K., and P. S. Chung. "Revelation and Scripture." In *Global Dictionary of Theology*, edited by William A. Dyrness and Veli-Matti Kärkkäinen, 758–67. Downers Gove, IL: InterVarsity, 2008.

Michel, Thomas F., editor and translator. *A Muslim Theologian's Response to Christianity: Ibn Taymiyya's Al-Jawab al-Sahih*. New York: Caravan, 1984.

Minear, Paul. *Images of the Church in the New Testament*. Louisville: Westminster John Knox, 2004.

Mingana, Alphonse. *The Apology of Timothy the Patriarch before the Caliph Mahdi*. Piscataway, NJ: Gorgias, 2009.

Mohamed, Besheer. "A New Estimate of the U.S. Muslim Population." Pew Research Center, January 6, 2016. http://www.pewresearch.org/fact-tank/2016/01/06/a-new-estimate-of-the-u-s-muslim-population/.

Morse, Christopher. *Not Every Spirit: A Dogmatics of Christian Disbelief*. 2nd ed. New York: Continuum, 2009.

Mosher, Lucinda, and David Marshall, editors. *The Community of Believers: Christian and Muslim Perspectives*. Washington, DC: Georgetown University Press, 2015.

Moucarry, Chawkat. *Faith to Faith: Christianity & Islam in Dialogue*. Leicester: InterVarsity, 2001.

Moussalli, Ahmad S. "Islamic Democracy and Pluralism." In *Progressive Muslims: On Justice, Gender, and Pluralism*, edited by Omid Safi, 286–305. Oxford: Oneworld, 2003.

Munir, Fareed. "Islam and Franciscanism: Prophet Mohammad of Arabia and St. Francis of Assisi in the Spirituality of Mission." *Spirit and Life: A Journal of Contemporary Franciscanism* 9 (2000) 25–42.

Murata, Sachiko, and William C. Chittick. *The Vision of Islam*. St. Paul, MN: Paragon House, 1994.

Nasr, Seyyed Hossein. "Comments on a Few Theological Issues in the Islamic-Christian Dialogue." In *Christian-Muslim Encounters*, edited by Yvonne Y. Haddad and Wadi Z. Haddad, 458–65. Gainesville: University of Florida Press, 1995.

———. *The Heart of Islam: Enduring Values for Humanity.* New York: Harper, 2002.

Neusner, Jacob. "Do Monotheist Religions Worship the Same God? A Perspective on Classical Judaism." In *Do Jews, Christians, and Muslims Worship the Same God?*, edited by Jacob Neusner et al., 25–53. Nashville: Abingdon, 2012.

Neusner, Jacob, et al. *Do Jews, Christians, and Muslims Worship the Same God?* Nashville: Abingdon, 2012.

Neuwirth, Angelika. *Der Koran als Text der Spätantike: ein europäisher Zugang.* Berlin: Verlag der Weltreligionen, 2010.

Nickel, Gordon. "Early Muslim Accusations of *Tahrif*: Muqatil ibn Sulayman's Commentary on Key Qur'anic Verses." In *The Bible in Arab Christianity*, edited by David Thomas, 207–23. Leiden: Brill, 2007.

———. *Narratives of Tampering in the Earliest Commentaries on the Qur'an.* Leiden: Brill, 2004.

Nogalski, James D. *The Book of the Twelve: Hosea-Jonah.* Macon, GA: Smyth & Helwys, 2011.

Nursi, Bediuzzaman Said. "The Sixteenth Letter." In *The Letters*, translated by Şükran Vahide. Rev. ed. Risale-i Nur Collection 2. Istanbul: Sölzer, 1997.

Nussbaum, Martha. *The New Religious Intolerance: Overcoming the Politics of Fear in an Anxious Age.* Cambridge, MA: Harvard University Press, 2012.

O'Collins, Gerald. *Interpreting Jesus.* Eugene, OR: Wipf & Stock, 2002.

Palombo, Cecilia. "The 'Correspondence' of Leo III and 'Umar II: Traces of an Early Christian Arabic Apologetic Work." *Millennium-Jahrbuch* 12/1 (2015) 231–64.

Patel, Eboo. *Sacred Ground: Pluralism, Prejudice, and the Promise of America.* Boston: Beacon, 2013.

Paul VI, Pope. *Ecclesiam suam* ("Paths of the Church"). Papal encyclical, August 6, 1964. http://w2.vatican.va/content/paul-vi/en/encyclicals/documents/hf_p-vi_enc_06081964_ecclesiam.html.

Penn, Michael Philip. *When Christians First Met Muslims: A Sourcebook of the Earliest Syriac Writings on Islam.* Oakland: University of California Press, 2015.

Pew Research Center. *The Future of World Religions: Population Growth Projections, 2010–2050.* April 2, 2015. http://www.pewforum.org/2015/04/02/religious-projections-2010-2050/.

———. *The Global Religious Landscape.* December 2012. http://www.pewforum.org/2012/12/18/global-religious-landscape-exec/.

———. "Who Knows What About Religion." In *U.S. Religious Knowledge Survey*, 16–36. September 28, 2010. http://www.pewforum.org/2010/09/28/u-s-religious-knowledge-survey-who-knows-what-about-religion/.

———. *The World's Muslims: Religion, Politics, and Society.* April 30, 2013. http://www.pewforum.org/2013/04/30/the-worlds-muslims-religion-politics-society-overview/.

Pickthall, Muhammad Marmaduke. "The Meaning of the Glorious Qur'an." In *The Qur'an*, edited by Jane McAuliffe, 3–356. New York: Norton, 2017.

Pohl, Christine D. *Making Room: Recovering Hospitality as a Christian Tradition.* Grand Rapids: Eerdmans, 1999.

Pratt, Douglas. *Christian Engagement with Islam: Ecumenical Journeys since 1910*. Leiden: Brill, 2017.

———. "Contextual Paradigms for Interfaith Relations." *Current Dialogue* 42 (December 2003) 3–9.

———. "Pluralism and Interreligious Engagement: The Contexts of Dialogue." In *A Faithful Presence: Essays for Kenneth Cragg*, edited by David Thomas with Clare Amos, 402–18. London: Melisende, 2003.

Prins, Baukje. *Voorbij de onschuld: het debat over integratie in Nederland*. Amsterdam: Van Gennep, 2004.

Prothero, Stephen. *God Is Not One*. San Francisco: HarperOne, 2011.

Provan, Iain. *1 and 2 Kings*. Peabody, MA: Hendrickson, 1995.

Rahner, Karl. "Einzigkeit und Dreifaltigkeit Gottes." In *Der Gott des Christentums und des Islam*, edited by Andreas Bsteh, 119–36. Mödling, Austria: Verlag St. Gabriel, 1978.

Ramadan, Tariq. *The Messenger: The Meanings of the Life of Muhammad*. London: Penguin, 2008.

Ratzinger, Joseph. *"In the Beginning . . .": A Catholic Understanding of the Story of Creation and the Fall*. Grand Rapids: Eerdmans, 1995.

Resnick, I. "The Falsification of Scripture and Medieval Christian and Jewish Polemics." *Medieval Encounters* 2/3 (1996) 344–80.

Reynolds, Gabriel Said. "On the Qur'anic Accusation of Scriptural Falsification (tahrif) and Christian Anti-Jewish Polemic." *Journal of the American Oriental Society* 130/2 (April–June 2010) 189–202.

———. *The Qur'an and its Biblical Subtext*. Oxon: Routledge, 2010.

Rhodes, Ron. *The 10 Things You Need to Know about Islam*. Eugene: Harvest House, 2007.

Ricoeur, Paul. *The Symbolism of Evil*. London: ET, 1967.

Robinson, Neil. *Christ in Islam and Christianity*. Albany: State University of New York Press, 1991.

Roggema, Barbara. "The Affair of the Death of Muhammad." In *Christian-Muslim Relations: A Bibliographical History, Volume 1 (600–900)*, edited by David Thomas and Barbara Roggema, 401–2. Leiden: Brill, 2009.

———. *The Legend of Sergius Bahira: Eastern Christian Apologetics and Apocalyptic in Response to Islam*. Leiden: Brill, 2009.

Rondet, Henri. *Original Sin: The Patristic and Theological Background*. Shannon: Ecclesia, 1972.

Roy, Olivier. *Globalised Islam: The Search for A New Ummah*. London: Hurst, 2004.

Saeed, Abdullah. "The Nature and Purpose of the Community (Ummah) in the Qur'an." In *The Community of Believers*, edited by Lucinda Mosher and David Marshall, 15–28. Washington, DC: Georgetown University Press, 2015.

Sahih al-Bukhari. https://www.sunnah.com.

Salem, Feryal. *The Emergence of Early Sufi Piety and Sunni Scholasticism: 'Abdallah B. Al-Mubarak and the Formation of Sunni Identity in the Second Islamic Century*. Leiden: Brill, 2016.

Samir, Samir Khalil. "The Earliest Arab Apology for Christianity (c. 750)." In *Christian Arabic Apologetics during the Abbasid Period (750–1258)*, edited by Samir Khalil Samir and Jørgen S. Nielsen, 57–114. Leiden: Brill, 1994.

Schmidtke, Sabine. "The Muslim Reception of Biblical Materials: Ibn Qutayba and His A'lam al-nubuwwa." *Islam and Christian-Muslim Relations* 22/3 (July 2011) 249–74.

Second Vatican Ecumenical Council. *Ad gentes* ["To the Nations"]: *On the Mission Activity of the Church*. December 7, 1965. http://www.vatican.va/archive/hist_councils/ii_vatican_council/documents/vat-ii_decree_19651207_ad-gentes_en.html.

———. *Gaudium et spes* ["Joy and Hope"]: *Pastoral Constitution on the Church in the Modern World*. December 7, 1965. http://www.vatican.va/archive/hist_countils/ii_vatican_council/documents/vat-ii_const_19651207_gaudium-et-spes_en.html.

———. *Lumen gentium* ["Light of the Nations"]: *Dogmatic Constitution on the Church*. November 21, 1964. http://www.vatican.va/archive/hist_councils/ii_vatican_council/documents/vat-ii_const_19641121_lumen-gentium_en.html.

———. *Nostra aetate* ["In Our Time"]: *Declaration on the Relation of the Church to Non-Christian Religions*. October 28, 1965. http://www.vatican.va/archive/hist_councils/ii_vatican_council/documents/vat-ii_decl_19651028_nostra-aetate_en.html.

Sen, Amartya. *Identity and Violence: The Illusion of Destiny*. New York: Norton, 2006.

al-Shalabi, Jamal. "The Amman Message: An Early Confrontation with Extremist Islamic Movements." In *Muslim Identity in a Turbulent Age: Islamic Extremism and Western Islamophobia*, edited by Mike Hardy, Fiyaz Mughal, and Sarah Markiewicz, 133–50. London: Jessica Kingsley, 2017.

Shenk, W. R. "Gospel." In *Global Dictionary of Theology*, edited by William A. Dyrness and Veli-Matti Kärkkäinen, 356–58. Downers Grove, IL: InterVarsity, 2008.

Siddiqui, Mona. *Christians, Muslims, and Jesus*. New Haven, CT: Yale University Press, 2013.

———, editor. *The Routledge Reader in Christian-Muslim Relations*. London: Routledge, 2013.

Sirry, Munim. *Scriptural Polemics: The Qur'an and Other Religions*. Oxford: Oxford University Press, 2014.

Sokolowski, Robert. *The God of Faith and Reason: Foundations of Christian Theology*. Notre Dame, IN: University of Notre Dame Press, 1982.

Swiddler, Leonard, et al. *Death or Dialogue?: From the Age of Monologue to the Age of Dialogue*. London: SCM, 1990.

al-Tabari, 'Ali Ibn Sahl Rabban. *The Polemical Works of 'Ali al-Tabari*, edited by Rifaat Ebeid and David Thomas. Leiden: Brill, 2016.

Taji-Farouki, Suha, editor. *Modern Muslim Intellectuals and the Qur'an*. Oxford: Oxford University Press, 2006.

Taylor, David G. K. "The Disputation between a Muslim and a Monk of Bet Hale: Syriac Text and Annotated English Translation." In *Christsein in der islamischen Welt: Festschrift für Martin Tamcke zum 60. Geburtstag*, edited by Sidney H. Griffith and Sven Grebenstein, 187–242. Wiesbaden: Harrassowitz Verlag, 2015.

Thackston, W. M., Jr., translator. *The Tales of the Prophets of al-Kisa'i*. Boston: Twayne, 1978.

Thomas, David. "Islam and the Religious Other." In *Understanding Interreligious Relations*, edited by David Cheetham, Douglas Pratt, and David Thomas, 148–71. Oxford: Oxford University Press.

Thiselton, Anthony C. *1 Corinthians: A Shorter Exegetical & Pastoral Commentary*. Grand Rapids: Eerdmans, 2006.

Tibi, Bassam. *Islam between Culture and Politics*. Basingstoke: Palgrave, 2001.

Tieszen, Charles. *Christian-Identity amid Islam in Medieval Spain*. Leiden: Brill, 2013.

———. *Cross Veneration in the Medieval Islamic World: Christian Identity and Practice under Muslim Rule*. London: I. B. Tauris, 2017.

————. *A Textual History of Christian-Muslim Relations: Seventh–Fifteenth Centuries.* Minneapolis: Fortress, 2015.

Toft, Monica Duffy, Daniel Philpott, and Timothy Samuel Shah. *God's Century: Resurgent Religion and Global Politics.* New York: Norton, 2011.

Tritton, Arthur Stanley. "The Speech of God." *Studia Islamica* 36 (1972) 5–22.

Troll, Christian W. *Dialogue and Difference: Clarity in Christian-Muslim Relations.* New York: Orbis, 2009.

————. "Muhammad—Prophet auch für Christen?" *Stimmen der Zeit*, May 2007, 291–303.

Vahide, Sukran. *Islam in Modern Turkey: An Intellectual Biography of Bediuzzaman Said Nursi.* New York: SUNY Press, 2005.

Valkenberg, Pim. "Can We Talk Theologically? Thomas Aquinas and Nicholas of Cusa on the Possibility of a Theological Understanding of Islam." In *Rethinking the Medieval Legacy for Contemporary Theology*, edited by Anselm K. Min, 131–66. Notre Dame, IN: University of Notre Dame Press, 1979.

————. "Christian Identity and Theology of the Trinity." In *Identity and Religion: A Multi-Disciplinary Approach*, edited by Ad Borsboom and Frans Jespers, 267–90. Saarbrücken: Verlag für Entwicklungspolitik, 2003.

————. "A Common Word or a Word of Justice? Two Qur'anic Approaches to Christian-Muslim Dialogue." In *Future of Interfaith Dialogue: Muslim-Christian Encounters through A Common Word*, edited by Lejla Demiri and Yazid Said. Cambridge: Cambridge University Press, forthcoming in 2018.

————. "God(s) of Abraham: Sibling Rivalry among Three Faiths." *The Christian Century* 133/14 (July 6, 2016) 28–31.

————. "*Nostra Aetate*: Historical Contingency and Theological Significance." In *Nostra Aetate: Celebrating 50 Years of the Catholic Church's Dialogue with Jews and Muslims*, edited by Pim Valkenberg and Anthony Cirelli, 6–26. Washington, DC: Catholic University of America Press, 2017.

Valkenberg, Pim, and Anthony Cirelli, editors. *Nostra Aetate: Celebrating 50 Years of the Catholic Church's Dialogue with Jews and Muslims.* Washington, DC: Catholic University of America Press, 2016.

Versteegh, Kees. *Landmarks in Linguistic Thought III: The Arab Linguistic Tradition.* London: Routledge, 1997.

Volf, Miroslav. *Allah: A Christian Response.* New York: HarperOne, 2011.

———— , editor. *Do We Worship the Same God? Jews, Christians, and Muslims in Dialogue.* Grand Rapids: Eerdmans, 2012.

Volf, Miroslav, Ghazi bin Muhammad, and Melissa Yarrington, editors. *A Common Word: Muslims and Christians on Loving God and Neighbor.* Grand Rapids: Eerdmans, 2010.

Wahlde, Urban C., von. *The Gospel and Letters of John.* Vol. 3: *Commentary on the Three Johannine Letters.* Grand Rapids: Eerdmans, 2010.

Waardenburg, Jacques. *Muslim Perceptions of Other Religions.* Oxford: Oxford University Press, 1999.

Wansbrough, John. *Qur'anic Studies: Sources and Methods of Scriptural Interpretation.* New York: Prometheus, 2004.

Ware, Timothy. *The Orthodox Church: An Introduction to Eastern Christianity.* London: Penguin, 2015.

Watt, William Montgomery. *The Formative Period of Islamic Thought.* Oxford: Oneworld, 2002.

Weisenfeld, Judith. *New World A-Coming: Black Religion and Racial Identity during the Great Migration*. New York: New York University Press, 2016.

Wild, Stefan. "Canon." In *The Quran: An Encyclopedia*, edited by Oliver Leaman, 136–39. Oxon: Routledge, 2006.

Wilde, Clare Elena. *Approaches to the Qur'an in Early Christian Arabic Texts (750–1258 CE)*. Washington, DC: Academica, 2014.

Wiley, Tatha. *Original Sin: Origins, Developments, Contemporary Meanings*. New York: Paulist, 2002.

Wiredu, Kwesi. *Cultural Universals and Particulars: An African Perspective*. Bloomington: Indiana University Press, 1996.

Wüstenfeld, F., and Dritter Band, editors. *Das Leben Muhammed's nach Muhammed Ibn Ishak bearbeitet von Abd el-Malik Ibn Hischam*. Gottingen: Dieterichsche Universitäts-Buchhandlung, 1858.

Yarnold, Edward. *The Theology of Original Sin*. Notre Dame, IN: Fides, 1971.

Zebiri, Kate. *Muslims and Christians Face to Face*. Oxford: Oneworld, 1997.

Zurlo, Gina A., and Todd M. Johnson. "Unaffiliated, Yet Religious: A Methodological and Demographic Analysis." In *Sociology of Atheism*, edited by Roberto Cipriani and Franco Garelli, 50–74. Leiden: Brill, 2016.